A Mother's Worth

By Carol Rigby

Trafford
PUBLISHING

Order this book online at www.trafford.com/08-0717
or email orders@trafford.com

Most Trafford titles are also available at major online book retailers.

Note for Librarians: A cataloguing record for this book is available from Library
and Archives Canada at www.collectionscanada.ca/amicus/index-e.html

Printed in Victoria, BC, Canada.

ISBN: 978-1-4251-8005-8

*We at Trafford believe that it is the responsibility of us all, as both individuals
and corporations, to make choices that are environmentally and socially sound.
You, in turn, are supporting this responsible conduct each time you purchase a
Trafford book, or make use of our publishing services. To find out how you are
helping, please visit www.trafford.com/responsiblepublishing.html*

*Our mission is to efficiently provide the world's finest, most comprehensive
book publishing service, enabling every author to experience success.
To find out how to publish your book, your way, and have it available
worldwide, visit us online at www.trafford.com/10510*

Trafford
PUBLISHING   www.trafford.com

North America & international
toll-free: 1 888 232 4444 (USA & Canada)
phone: 250 383 6864 ♦ fax: 250 383 6804 ♦ email: info@trafford.com

The United Kingdom & Europe
phone: +44 (0)1865 487 395 ♦ local rate: 0845 230 9601
facsimile: +44 (0)1865 481 507 ♦ email: info.uk@trafford.com

10 9 8 7 6 5 4

DEDICATION

To Linda, Katrina, Joanna, Heather and Jennifer, the mothers of my grandchildren and future grandchildren and to all mothers everywhere for the great and important work they do.

Also to my husband Michael who has been to me and to our six children a constant example of love and self-mastery.

Your child needs your example as their mother; they need to see you live your life as fully and as well as you can. When you do this you give your child an expectation that they too can have a fullness of life and achievement.

CONTENTS

Introduction   7

Part One Strategies and Tools   13

   Chapter One A Mother's Worth   15

   Chapter Two Who Am I and What Do I Value?   20

   Chapter Three I Believe in Myself   30

   Chapter Four Visualise Your Future   39

   Chapter Five Affirm Your Success   46

   Chapter Six The Power of Habit   52

Part Two How the Mind Works   61

   Chapter Seven The Mind, Spirit and Body   62

   Chapter Eight Six Mind Muscles   71

   Chapter Nine Seven Steps To Self-Mastery   84

   Chapter Ten Spiritual or Universal Laws   99

Part Three Create Your Future   107

   Chapter Eleven Present State to Desired State   109

   Chapter Twelve Plan of Happiness   118

   Chapter Thirteen Appreciate 'You'   127

INTRODUCTION

As a mother you are the most important person in your child's world, everything you do and say will have some kind of an impact upon them and they will form their own image of the world from your image and perception of life in your world. This book is written from my experience of life and how I influenced my children, now my children are grown I see things in them that I know they inherited from me.

When we look around our communities we can see there is a great need for us to find ways to inspire and motivate our children and as a mother you can do that by inspiring and motivating yourself to be the best you can be. Improving your life and developing your potential will also help your children to do the same because they will learn from your example.

This is your book; it acknowledges the great work that you do and the fact that you are doing the toughest job in the world with no training and no annual income. It is written to lift and inspire you to be the best you can be. The world needs you and other mothers like you, who know who they are and who love themselves and treat themselves with kindness and respect. You as a mother can develop your own ability to think and feel good about yourself and your child, and in return your child will find they can give their children the needed love, attention and guidance they deserve.

A child can struggle with the demands of education or the lack of education, with the mass of advertising and the ever-growing peer pressure to have, be, or do certain things. Mother and child need each other more than at any time and it is you, the mother, who can take control of the situation and take the responsibility to arm yourself with the knowledge, courage and confidence it will take to turn around the social unrest that is at large in the country today. No longer can you, as a mother, turn a blind eye because it could be your child that is the next one to get injured or die.

The purpose of this book is to allow you to develop your personal self and to gain power over your own life and in turn give that power to your child. As a mother you are the most important person in your child's world and also to your family, community and country. As you develop your understanding and your skills you will grow in wisdom until you become the greatest role model your child has.

Every child born into this life needs a role model, someone who can show by example, what this life is and how to live in such a way that they in turn become role models to their children and so the cycle of life goes on.

In today's world there is a problem and a challenge when it comes to a child learning from role models. Some generations ago life in the western world started to change, it was called progress, people started to recognise that they had a choice in life and that they could exercise that choice and certain authority did not have to be followed. After the Second World War there was a great need for people to help build the country again, life had been on hold for six long years.

Life started to change and people started to realize that they had ability. Men who had served in the war had experiences where they had to dig deep into their own inner resources to survive. Women too, had to find hidden reservoirs of strength and ability to deal with the experiences they had encountered. During my early life in the 1950's I remember mothers pushing their boys to be the best they could be in school if they wanted an apprenticeship at Rolls Royce and not have to work in the coalmines.

The point is that people began to realise that they had choice, after generations of class division and certain people holding authority over others. Those 'others' decided that they had a choice and that they did not have to conform to the opinions and rules of someone else. This brought about the flower power movement and more love and consideration for peoples' feelings and choice was recognised. Individuals took it into their own mind that they could develop and create their own life according to their own desires.

This was a great movement and many people succeeded in living their lives their way. As with any change in attitude it has its potential for good and bad and some of the good came with the freedom to choose and to become equal to each other. It gave people the opportunity to develop their own potential and ability, which was good and necessary.

The unfortunate side effect of this movement was that although boys were encouraged to work hard and to be the best they could be, it was my experience that the girls, the mothers to be, were given the impression that they did not need an education. They needed to learn how to be a homemaker, how to look after these boys who would become their husbands, they did not need exams and apprenticeships. Girls would go to school and then leave, work in a textile factory for a few years, get married, and have children, their lives would then be dedicated to caring for their children, and if necessary their aging parents.

This conditioned thinking gave mothers the impression and belief that they were not important; that they had no value, yet the job they were doing was the most important job in the world. Through the succeeding generations this conditioned thinking has been perpetuated and today we can see that we have a generation of mothers who generally do feel undervalued and have no direction in their own lives because of the lack of direction and values missing from their childhood, and also a positive role model.

For 50 years generation after generation of children have had less and less direction in life to help them to live and have control over their own circumstances. Parents struggle to keep up with the ever-increasing demands of modern day living and now it is coming to crisis point. Children are killing children; children are having and raising children

Studying this book will help you to find the necessary knowledge and understanding of yourself. You can then pass this onto your children and help them to feel the love and security that comes from knowing who they are and what they can achieve if they will make the effort to train their own minds to think.

You are what you think, and if you think you are great you will be great, if you think you are no one, you will be no one. Law governs your life upon this earth and these laws are irrevocable, that means they cannot be changed and they work for everyone in the same way. Whether you are rich or poor, black or white it matters not, you are governed by these laws and to know and understand the law is advantageous to all people.

One of those laws is the law of cause and effect, meaning if you put your hand in fire (the cause) you will get burned (the effect). The result will be inevitable. It doesn't matter who you are you will get burned. There is no privilege with these laws, they do not recognise division of any kind they only recognise obedience or disobedience and give the appropriate result.

As a mother you are important to the child because you can teach these laws and obedience of them to your child. From the minute of birth your child is learning and accepting life as it comes to them. If they are to function in life with any degree of success, they need teaching about the laws and also need good examples to help them to choose their way through childhood, developing values and direction along the way.

When you as a mother know who you are, and what you stand for, you are more able to advise your child of what they need to know, who they are, and what they stand for. It is my express desire to give you, a mother, that knowledge and understanding you need to be the good role model to your child and that in turn will help the child to grow up with respect for itself and also for everyone else.

Freedom of choice is still a great thing and so is happiness and many people end up forfeiting happiness because of their choices. To be able to choose wisely, a person needs to understand the consequence that comes with the choice they make and you can give this to your child.

The mother is the best person to do this and you can do it early in your child's life. Do it before your child is influenced by outside forces, which may lead to undesirable living and bring on life long unhappiness. You really are the most important person in your child's life and you need to develop the necessary skills and understanding to give your child the best start in life. As your child grows and the cycle of life continues, then your child will become a good role model to their children and with each generation we will have stronger and more disciplined people playing their part in society, making the world a happy and peaceful place in which to live.

Many times in this age in which we live you are told what to think but not how to think and how to use the mind to create the life you desire. Your greatest asset is not your body, it is your mind, and when you learn how to use your mind your life will change in accordance to the effort you give to the change you desire.

Your life is made up of the habits you have developed over a period of time; these habits actually control your life and become your actions or reactions. Doing or thinking something over and over again until the sub-conscious accepts it as normal forms a habit. When a situation arises, you do not have to think of what to do every time, your habit in that particular situation will take over, and you will react to it in your usual way.

When you are doing something that you do regularly on a daily basis, like driving a car, you do not have to think every time of every little action you need to take, they become habitual and you do them automatically. It is the same with anything in life. Your reactions to recognised situations will be habitual. We must ask ourselves if these habits are wise, or do we need to reassess them?

The physical cravings of the body direct your life and that is when you become a prisoner to the passions and appetites of your physical body. These cravings have come through habit; you have conditioned your body and mind to react in a certain way to a certain situation. To learn to develop your thinking and feeling will greatly enhance your life by gaining control over your physical appetites and focusing your efforts upon creating a life that will bring you the happiness and peace of mind you desire for yourself and your children.

As you study this book let it work upon your mind, let it create you by putting into action the teachings. Remember you are the most important person to your child and also to your family, community and country. Let that importance show by making the changes you need to make no matter how small. They will have an effect.

Choose to be your child's role model, take control of your own life and affect your child's life in a way that will help him/her to become an adult who has control of his/her own mind and happiness. The world needs mothers who know who they are and what they are about, mothers who have the confidence to act and to stand up and be counted as doing the greatest and most important job in the world.

No politician can have the effect you can have on leading and changing the world. You have the greatest opportunity to develop yourself and your child and future children by changing your own life to be one that is great and happy. One that works with the laws of the universe to bring about the life you would live and have your child live.

I call upon you now to get up and be counted, to feel the passion for excellence within you, it does not matter who you are now it only matters who you decide you will become. Start from wherever you are now, and make one small change today and another small change tomorrow and before long you will notice a great difference in you and in your children.

I wish you well in your journey; it will be one of challenge, rise to the challenge, stay focused upon your desire and keep reaching for the goals you set yourself. You are worth the effort it takes to take control of your thoughts and your life. Continue even when you make a mistake, see mistakes for what they are, learning experiences, learn from them and move on, do not give up at each hurdle, work to get over or around them. You are unique and special; each mother will make a difference and you can!

Part One

∞

STRATEGIES AND TOOLS

HUMANS were created to progress and every mother contains within herself the capacity for continued development. To advance in all things is life's greatest purpose and by learning to work within the laws you can promote that aim, as a mother you may build yourself into greater and greater success.

If you examine the processes of nature you will find only success. Nature knows no failures; her plans are about success and she aims at those results in every form and manner. To succeed in the best and the fullest sense of the term you, as a mother must aim at success and recognise any result you get, good or bad, as feedback to learn from and not as failure.

Nature uses all the resources around her and you also have resources that are at your disposal. There are no limits to your possibilities; you can focus on the individual elements, forces, and principles of the world. You can develop a wonderful intelligence. This will help to answer many questions which you previously did not recognise as such and you will find that what seemed impossible becomes possible.

By using the strategies and tools within this book you will release dormant powers within you, enabling you to awaken your faculties, talents and insight. Your mind will develop greatness it is simply a matter of knowing how. True self-help, self-discovery, self-knowledge, and the proper instruction in applying your mind and using your own mind muscles will advance you as a person. As you practise you will ensure efficiency; and you will achieve results and success. It is within your reach if you aspire to it.

Do you wish to succeed? You can! You possess all you need within yourself; all you need is to gain a clear understanding of the principles and laws upon which success is based, and then to apply the right methods of operating these causes until success is earned.

Chapter One

∽

A MOTHER'S WORTH

MANY years ago Sir Winston Churchill gave a stirring quote about fighting on the landing strips and on the beaches to protect our country and our freedom. That quote lifted and inspired the people of the United Kingdom to come together and to fight for the freedom of the nation. Now again today there is need of a rallying cry that will inspire and lift the mothers of this country to fight for the freedom of their children and themselves, not from the threat of an invading army but a freedom from the metaphorical prison bars that surround people who have not been taught. People who do not know how to use their minds and their abilities to build lives of freedom to live in the circumstances to which they aspire.

How important you are in today's society. You are unfortunately the most often forgotten and dismissed of people. It is easy to forget you because there is no immediate panic in the company or country. When a mother becomes ineffective, it is felt only in the home, where the results of a missing mum are not felt until much later.

What happens to a home when the mother is gone, has an illness or is not working effectively and cannot fulfil her role as mother, what disappears in the organisation, the housekeeper, the cook, the first aider, the production staff, the company accountant, the buyer, and many other positions which a company could not perform without?

On a smaller scale every family in the country is like a manufacturing company and what they are producing is the leaders and workers of tomorrow. Tomorrows' mothers, fathers, bankers, politicians, managing directors, accountants, doctors, nurses, builders, plumbers, electricians and many more people that the country will need to develop to become a place fit for a race of people to inhabit.

It is imperative that the country and the mothers themselves recognise the worth of a mother and no matter how old, young, rich or poor each mother must lift her head high and come to know the importance of the work she is performing 24 hours a day for love.

In monetary terms there is no salary. Your salary as a mother comes in the love and respect you feel from the very people you are working with and just as a good leader will gain the respect of the people they are leading so will a mother gain the love and respect of her children as she leads and guides them through the difficult maze of life and all the different paths that will be open to them.

> **"The hand that rocks the cradle rules the world,"**
> ANONYMOUS

This proverb really is true and it shows how, you as a mother, are important in your role in society. When a society starts to breakdown it is you as a mother that can take a hold of it and build it back up again. You can take control of your company and communicate with it, to start to notice if there is a problem in your area. This will take some focused attention on your part and also recognition of your part in the breakdown of your company.

Look around at society there is a great need for someone to notice that we have a breakdown in many companies. There is a problem with leadership, communication, respect for authority and the ability to work and you need to take control of this before it bankrupts the company and leaves everyone redundant.

How can you tackle such a complex and difficult situation when it is so widespread and damaging that it is making life intolerable for some and stopping them from performing normally in their own company? Each company has a leader, a manager, the person who is in control or who should be in control. Just as in a company a leader will be in control of what happens in their company, so in a family you the mother can take control of what is happening in your family.

As an aside I do not mention fathers here because the focus of this book is upon the role of a mother and your part in keeping control of your company, the father too has a very important role to play but it is the mother's role that keeps the day to day running of the company smooth and effective.

Leading Effectively

How does a mother lead effectively especially if there is already a real problem within the company (family)? Just as any good leader will tell you it is important to have the ear of your people and for a mother that is your child. When you can get them to listen to you and to hear you and respect what you are saying then you will find that they will follow your lead and you will start to take control.

This will not come from a dictatorship, although you may find they will obey because they are afraid or because they do not want the consequences of not obeying. A dictator will never gain the total respect of their people because eventually someone will lead a takeover and overcome the dictator. A good leader will win the respect of their people by communicating with them in a way that makes their people feel good about themselves and helps them to grow and learn.

As a mother you are the heart of your organisation and out of that heart can come all the love you need to lead and guide your child and to help your child become the person who will grow up and lead and guide their own companies with love and respect for their people.

As a mother you are the most important person in your family and if you are not working effectively you cannot do what it takes to lead and guide your child. If you do not value yourself and your status as a mother then you will not lead effectively and your child will suffer because of it. So ask yourself, 'what do I want as a mother?' 'Do I want to be in control of my own life so I can be effective in guiding my child to be happy and to achieve the best that is in them?'

You can be the greatest influence on your child, you can be their rock and their safety net, a place where they can come when life is difficult and they need some guidance and love to help them through it. Your child will come to you if they know they can rely upon you to help them to feel good about who they are and give them the direction they need to know what to do. Just as in a company department the workers look to the manager for direction and it is when that manager is not giving direction that the problems start.

If, as a mother you are to give direction, you need to have some direction yourself, you need to know who you are and what you want to achieve so that you can communicate this effectively to your child. A good way to start and find your own direction is to start asking yourself some questions; asking questions of yourself will help you to look within yourself for the answers. It is no good looking anywhere else to find out what you want, it is all within you, no programme or magazine article will give you the answers to the questions you ask yourself, they can only come from within you.

What questions can you ask, some good ones could be 'Who am I?' When you ask that question and focus on it long enough you will start to recognise what values you have in life and when you know what values you have you will gain some direction in your own life. Another question could be 'What do I want?' If you do not know what you want how can you possibly achieve it, you will go on meandering through life never getting and achieving what is within you. What about asking yourself 'Why do I want it?' Knowing why you want something is important because if you know who you are and what you want and you start on the path to getting it, you will soon come up against barriers that you will need to get over or around and it is knowing why you are doing what you are doing that will give you the perseverance and tenacity to stick to your task.

As a mother whatever your status, working outside the home or whether you are at home full time you need to know and feel your own importance within your family. If you have a husband or partner then you can share some of the responsibility and also have someone else to work with and talk to in deciding the direction of your family.

If you are a mother working alone then you will need to be the one who is leading and guiding your child and you will need to know more than anyone how important your role is. It does not matter where you are now, whether you feel you have good control and direction or whether you feel you have no control at all, from this moment on you are in control and in the following pages we will discuss and show you how you can take control and win the hearts and love of your children so they will listen to you and follow your lead.

Your child needs you, if they do not get their direction and values from you they will get them from somewhere else. Do you want to take that chance that who ever is teaching your child and has the ear of your child will teach them the values and give them the direction you would like them to have. For the sake of your family it is worth learning and practising new ways of communicating and leading because no matter how old your child and what they are doing they will respond to your love if it is given unconditionally.

Put on your mantle of mother, wear it with pride and feel the love and the power that comes with that mantle. The power is a power that takes in all the tender feelings of a mother whose greatest desire is to see her child happy and walking in paths that are leading to achievement and security. Stand erect, hold your head high and look the world in the eye and know that as a mother you can succeed because of your undying love for your child. See that child as the person that has feelings and a tender heart and a mind that takes in all that it sees, hears, touches smells and tastes and from this information makes assumptions about their world. You have the opportunity to ensure their experience of the world is a good one.

Chapter Two

◎

WHO AM I AND WHAT DO I VALUE?

So much can be learned from the heritage of the people of this country that fought for its freedom; during the second World War Sir Winston Churchill gave praise about how so much was owed, by so many , to so few. Here he was talking about the Airmen who flew their planes with the constant challenge of mortal danger.

Let us look at the quote and instead of airmen put mothers, and even though the odds are daunting and the challenge constant, they can turn the tide in the plight of their children. Never in the field of mothering will so many children owe so much to their mothers, and every home in the country will be grateful that mothers took the courage and the determination to love and train their child to be good well rounded citizens who make the country a great place to live.

Just like the men and women who worked and fought for the freedom of this country, mothers can do the same with the same enthusiasm and passion that will let their light shine and guide the way for others. Do not be afraid to stand up and be counted, your child will thank you for it and will benefit greatly from your example. Everything you need is within you already; you just don't know it is there yet. You can find the answers to everything within you so may I suggest that you find a time when you can turn off the TV, radio or even a child and have some time when it is just you and the silence. If that means waiting until the child goes to bed then do that but do not try to do this exercise until you can have total time to yourself.

Now that you have the time and the silence ask yourself the question 'Who Am I?' and let it sink into your mind, ask it over and over and then listen to what comes into your mind. You may come up with some things like, I am a woman, I am a mother, I am honest, I am hardworking, I am loving, I am kind, I am strong.

All these things that you are coming up with are the things you value within you and they are the things that will guide and direct you in controlling your own life and guiding the life of your child. Your character is built upon the things that you value, some of the basic values of living a happy life might include Love, Kindness, Honesty, Gratitude, Integrity, Work, Patience and Morality.

By having these sorts of values you are building your life and character upon a solid foundation that will lead and guide you in your life and in turn will lead and guide your child. Your values will help you make decisions about what you will and won't do in your life and that will make life easier for you and the people around you, like your family.

You say you are honest, honesty is a value and, if you are honest with yourself and with others you will expect honesty to come back to you. Being honest with your child will help them to know they can rely upon you to be there for them, always recognising the good in them and helping them to be honest with themselves. Being honest does not mean that you have to be honest about the faults and failings of your child, sometimes you have to let them go and focus upon the good things your child does. When you are honest with someone you will tell him or her when he or she is good and when you feel they have excelled in something. It will be difficult for a person to grow to their potential unless they are given the praise and the motivation to do so and no one needs that more than a child. So being honest will mean telling someone when you feel they have done well, or even if they have not done so well you can be honest about the parts they did do well and build upon that.

Values are intangible, which means you cannot touch them, they are not solid objects, they are emotional traits that will lead and guide you in your life. If asked what you value you may say that you value your family which is a tangible thing, it is what your family means to you that you value. Your family is a tangible thing that you can touch but you may value the love or security that the family gives you, the love and security are the real values, and they are the emotional trait that having a family gives you.

You may say you value a car or money which again are tangible things so ask yourself what is it that a car or money give me. A car can give the freedom to travel, it is the freedom that you value, money can give security, success and status and they are the values that you hold.

Why are values important to you and, why it is worth spending time finding out what your values are and where they are leading you in your life? When you are doing this you may find that some values you have are negative and limit your potential to progress to become the person you want to become.

A negative value can be such traits as anger, jealousy, idleness and pride. These values can hold you back and also cause you much unhappiness if they are allowed to rule your life. The value of anger can limit your communication with other people especially your child, they will be afraid to talk with you about their feelings because of the response they may get.

If you do have anger as a value ask yourself what it is giving you in your life and is it good and helpful or is it hurting you and your relationships? Having jealousy as a value can really limit relationships and limit any happiness you may be able to feel. Also pride can be hard on you; if people feel they cannot speak freely with you because they may hurt your pride then you will become more and more isolated as the people around you will be wary of upsetting you. Idleness as a value can drain your life of energy and enthusiasm, it can limit you to the sofa and doing whatever activities can be done from wherever you are sitting or lying.

Your physical body, your thoughts and your emotions are all connected and when one is active the others become active. For instance if your physical body is moving and active your thoughts will be active and so will your emotions. It is hard to feel some positive emotion if you are sat on a sofa doing nothing, your thoughts may be ones of 'I don't care' or 'I am too tired' and your emotions will respond to this by feeling tired or careless and in turn your body will display tiredness and a posture of not caring about how you look or act.

Positive values can help you to feel alive and happy, they can direct your life along a path of achievement and success, and in contrast your negative values can hold you bound in a pattern of behaviour that is hard to break out of and to control. If you see negative values within your child you will probably find that you have the same negative values that they have learned from you, your example is your child's greatest learning experience.

From the moment your child is born they see your example and the way you live and they take that as being the way life is and the way to live. What a responsibility you have and that is why it is good to take the time to see what you value and how you can strengthen your positive values so that your child can get a positive role model and not a negative one.

Think about how you would like your child to act and live and then act and live that way yourself. If you want your child to be pleasant and kind you will need to be pleasant and kind to them and they will learn that pleasantness and kindness are good things to do because they feel good and you do them.

As a mother your greatest work will be with the child you love and in today's world it is so easy to let others do your job for you, the problem with that is they may not do the job of raising your child as you would like them to. One of these others who you may let into your mothering is the media, today the media is everywhere and comes into the home in many forms from TV, computers and computer games, magazines, radio and CD's and DVD's. How can you ensure that what your child is learning is what you want them to learn?

Spending time with your child and knowing what they are watching, reading and listening to will not only help you to know what is entertaining them and teaching them it will also show your child you are interested in them and what they are doing. If you are with the child you can monitor what is affecting their life and teach them what is good and what is bad for them. Your child needs this guidance and they will be grateful for it because it will give them a solid foundation on which to build their life and character.

As you observe your child and yourself you will find opportunities to teach, if something comes on TV that impresses itself upon your mind for good or bad you can be sure it will have an affect upon your child's mind and can be a perfect moment to teach a value to your child. Look for these opportunities everyday and take the time to teach your child about life and how you can live it so that it brings peace of mind and happiness.

Some of the things you can teach yourself and your child at these times is the difference between right and wrong. You can discuss with them the consequences of making good and bad choices and if they have made a bad choice act quickly to administer the consequence or allow the consequence to happen. Protecting your child from the consequences of their choices will not help them to develop the values and character that you envisage for them. They will need to know that their choices will always have a consequence and as they get older and more independent they will be able to make wise choices and be happy because of your time, teaching and example to them.

There is no greater joy for you than to see your child growing up happy and developing characteristics that enable them to have a life that has direction and progress. Your child will grow toward your expectations but if they do not know what you expect of them they will gradually find their own path through life, and that could be a dangerous way to go because their expectations will have come from outside sources. When you know what you value and want in life it will be so much easier to pass this on to your child, spend time with them discussing their future and make plans for it, ask them about their interests and ambitions, show confidence in their ability to make decisions for themselves. Talk about the values they have learned in the home and identify how these values will help them in their future life and help them to set goals to achieve.

As you do this with your child you will find that you are learning new things about yourself as well, you are learning that you are far more than you ever thought you were, your confidence in your ability as a mother will grow and you will start to feel the joy of mothering and the value you are to your family and to society. You will find pleasure in your family that will give you much happiness and peace of mind, you will know that your child is strong and can withstand the daily pressure of outside influences.

Your confidence as a mother will grow daily as you start to work on this, start now from wherever you are, observe what is happening in your own home and determine that what is happening is what you want to happen. This may seem like a big task when looked upon as a whole and you may feel overwhelmed by it. Break it down into smaller pieces; first of all just decide to spend more time with your child letting them feel your love and concern for them. As you spend time with them you will find natural opportunities to teach them, gently take those opportunities and teach them the things you value that will build good character. If someone is being mean and unkind on the TV ask him or her how that makes him or her feel and how the person he or she are being mean to feels. This is getting them to experience feelings in a safe environment and to understand the importance of other people in their life and that they have feelings too.

Doing small things like this on a daily basis will have a great affect on your life and the way you feel about yourself, it will also create within your home a feeling of love and harmony that will bring peace and happiness into your life. It does not matter now as an adult what happened for you in your childhood home, you have your own home your own child and your own values, you can decide what you want to happen. You have the freedom to choose and if you choose something different to your parents that is okay if it is inline with the values you have chosen to build your life upon.

It is not always easy to show love and affection to another person, even your child, especially if they are older and you are not used to being so open with them. Take it slowly, first of all let them know how much you love them by being there for them when they need you, as you work through challenges and experience life together you will find that you naturally feel affection, how you show that affection is personal and will come to you a little at a time. Spending time with someone is a great way to express your feelings for him or her because they know you care about them and want to be with them.

Going back to the question 'Who Am I?' you are the values you have in your life, they are your character and your direction, your values are the foundation for all the decisions you make in life so be sure you know what you value. You will enjoy your life so much more when you have a direction in which you are travelling. When a river meanders through the countryside it can look pretty and beautiful, it is not the same with a life, when a life is meandering it is going first this way and then that way, looking for the way of least resistance, this can be very tiring and exhausting, besides very confusing for yourself and for those around you. It can lead to an unstable life built upon a very soft foundation that could crumble at any moment.

Decide what your values are and live by them, through your example teach them to your child and enjoy the fruits of your labour as you enjoy a peaceful and happy family life.

Positive Values

Acceptance	Achievements	Adventure	Affection
Ambition	Comfort	Compassion	Contribution
Excitement	Freedom	Happiness	Honesty
Humour	Independence	Integrity	Intelligence
Intimacy	Kindness	Justice	Life Balance
Love	Loyalty	Passion	Power
Respect	Security	Sincerity	Spirituality
Success	Trust	Understanding	Wealth

Mean Values

Family	Car	House	Job		
Health	Mobile	Phone	Business	Money	

Negative Values

Anger	Apathy	Criticism	Dishonesty
Doubt	Fear	Jealousy	Hate
Idleness	Judgmental	Misery	Inconsistency
Rejection	Spite		

Out of the list of values above or any other values you may have that are not listed choose eight positive ones that are most important to you and then list those eight order of importance to you. This will give you the eight values that you live by and that affect all your decisions.

Example:
Compassion, Contribution, Health, Humour, Intelligence, Love, Loyalty, Spirituality.
The above eight values are what I have chosen as important and now I will put them in order of importance.

Spirituality
Happiness

Love
Compassion
Health
Loyalty
Contribution
Humour

Spirituality is my number one value, it is the part of my life that is important to me, as I nurture my spirit within me I build up my resilience and strength to be the person I really am deep within me. This allows me to know and feel what I need to do each day to achieve happiness.

Happiness is my next most important value, it is not the giddy, temporary feeling of excitement but a strong sense of well being and peace that comes with knowing that I am living my life the best I can and that no matter what happens my happiness will remain intact.

To love and to be loved is very important to me, I would find a life without love very hard indeed, and I sacrifice much of my time and life to give love and to receive love from my family and friends.

Compassion is something that has always been in me, my heart is touched very easy by the need of another and I will do my best to fill that need.

Without my health I could not give as freely and frequently as I do, I value being able to live each day with little thought of illness and limiting health circumstances.

Loyalty is a value that I taught my children, to be loyal to each other. I first came across loyalty when I was in my first year at senior school and through opening my mouth I got myself into bother and I was faced with this threat of a fight, my older sister came in and took the fight for me. I learned about loyalty from this experience, and I also learned to keep my mouth closed and to respect other peoples' opinions.

Contribution is important to me; it is what inspires me and lifts my motivation. When I can make a difference to someone in their life or to a community then I feel I have contributed.

Life would be so dull without humour, it is important to feel joy and happiness in life, it is important to interact with others in a humourous way and to socialize. It is how we develop relationships and enjoy life.

These are the most important values in my life, there are others of course that come after this list like intelligence and success and many others, it is the above that are the top eight that direct my life and help me to make decisions that affect me and my family.

When you know what you want and why you want it you are 50% of the way to having it. Take the time to get to know yourself and how you really feel about the world around you. Start to notice how you feel about what is happening around you whether it be in your real life or on a TV program, do not let your time in this world just pass you by, do not just be entertained by events of others, listen to and feel with the people around you or the characters on the program, see what it is that stirs up within you and ask yourself what you might do in a similar situation. As you do this you will start to recognize your own values and your ability to live by those values. Choose eight values that are most important to you and start to let those values direct your life and develop your relationships with your child and others around you.

As you come to know and practice the values that are important to you, your child will see your example and will learn how important it is to know what you value and how your values in life will help as you live by them and how important they are in knowing who you are and where you are going.

If you value justice you will find yourself moved by this value when you feel injustice is happening around you and you will maybe find yourself getting involved. Listen to this within you and ask yourself how you can best help to make sure justice is served in a way that ensures all parties learn and grow from the situation.

You are your child's lifeline to the outside world, what they see you doing they will think is right because you are the most important person in their world. You have a great responsibility as a mother to love and nurture your child, to give your child everything it needs to grow strong and healthy not just physically but also emotionally. Your child will cry when they are hungry and you will fill that need, it is easy to recognise that need in your child.

What is not so easy is the emotional needs of your child, they are crying out when they need their emotional needs met but it is not always a physical cry sometimes it comes in the way of their behaviour. If your child is showing behaviour that is causing them to get into trouble there may be an emotional need that is not being met, it could be that they need to feel your love and are trying to get your attention through their behaviour.

To be a mother is the greatest opportunity in the world but it is not the easiest. You do not need a university degree in maths or any other subject to do it, you need a degree of love, a massive degree of love and as you let this love build and grow within you and let it pour out of you into your family and others around you, your child will also feel this love and they also will let it fill them and pour out of them.

Love is the greatest power in the world, it can have far greater an effect than any nuclear power and it is freely available to any who will nurture it within them and give it to others.

As a mother you are part of the greatest movement on the earth, it is you that makes the world go around, as the world goes around so does life, it goes in cycles and the cycle of mothering can change the world and make it a wonderful place to be. Work in your world and change your world and as every other mother works to change her world the whole world will change for the better.

Chapter Three

❀

I BELIEVE IN MYSELF

Having decided who you are and what you stand for you will now need to develop your own self belief, that is to have the knowledge and emotional well being that you can go forward in your own life and achieve all that your heart desires. Being able to do this will be the greatest example to your child and will help them to develop their own self-belief and in turn create the life they desire for themselves.

As I have said earlier the most important thing you can do is to keep asking yourself questions that will cause you to go within yourself to find the answers and the big question on this page is to ask yourself, 'Are my beliefs about myself limiting me or helping me to grow?' Only you can answer this question and it will take time spent in quiet self-examination to effectively know what you believe about yourself and to take hold of your own life and beliefs and change what needs changing so you can feel the power that comes from within you when you have great self-belief.

Herbert Hoover who lived between the years of 1874 – 1964 and became a US President warned of the danger of developing a cult of mediocrity or in other words an acceptance of what is.

I am not sure when in his life he gave this warning but if you know he died in 1964 which is over 40 years ago you will know that this cult has been developing over the last few decades and has reached epic proportions. How many of you sit back and accept the life you have, feeling that this is it, this is my lot and I have to accept it and you never even try to climb up and out of it because you do not realise that there is a way out.

Why do you feel this way, what is it that has made you feel that you cannot do anything to move your life in a different direction that will give you that which you desire and that which you deserve. Look at the very last word of the quote, MEDIOCRITY, what does it mean, I looked it up in a dictionary and this is what I found.

'Ordinariness as a consequence of being average and not outstanding.'

Or a second description

'A person of second-rate ability, "A team of ageing second raters."

How does this make you feel as a person, do you want to be second rate or do you want to shine and lead the people you have responsibility for, your children. It is your choice, you can be average and meander through life never feeling the brilliance of achievement or you can be outstanding and let your light shine for your child and others around you.

Life is about having a choice, you can choose to believe in yourself and let your light shine and become the person you feel deep within you or you can choose to stay small and safe in your zone.

Take sometime now to feel your own brilliance in something, focus on something you are good at; let the feeling build within you until you feel good. Many times we focus on the things we cannot do and that makes us feel mediocre or even worse, no good. We even compare ourselves to others by our weaknesses and their strengths and wonder why we feel bad about ourselves.

Build yourself up by talking in positive terms about yourself and who you are, believe that you can achieve your dreams and goals. You have it within you to excel at something and as you do you will have a positive affect upon others around you.

As a mother those others in your life will be your family, as you believe in yourself and let your light shine in whatever way, your child will see that they too can let their light shine and they will develop their self belief and confidence and go on to achieve in their own life and to have the success they desire and deserve all because you decided that you were somebody and you let your light shine.

You can see that as a mother you have a tremendous impact on your child, if you have aspirations for your child, if you want them to have more than you had then you will need to stand up and be counted for what you believe in. To find some cause that you can work at and develop your abilities through, this does not mean that you need to spend countless hours outside the home; you can do this working with your own child. You can develop your ability to think, your mind is the most powerful part of you, you can have great physical power but it will be nothing without the power of the mind to direct your physical power.

Let us go back for another look at that word mediocrity and examine something else about it. Look at the first part of the word 'medio' it comes very close to the word 'media' and this is one of the biggest shifts in life you will have to make, to not let the media decide your life for you.

The media comes into modern day living very strongly, it is all around you all the time, you are bombarded by other peoples' opinions of what is. Advertising is a very strong cult in today's society and it is very persuasive, your child sees what is happening to others and they are affected by it. They will see someone in a magazine who may be skinny and dressed great and they want that, if they cannot have it, it makes them feel mediocre, average, second class or whatever you want to call it.

If you are also affected in this way, by the media, then this will have a double impact upon your child because they feel it from the media and they feel it from you too. Whatever you read, see or hear in the media is someone else's opinion, it is not truth, every person living is unique, different, and there can be no one way that is right, there is no one path that everyone should follow, everyone has their own path, so let the media go, do not be bound by it and its opinions. Your child will be much happier and better prepared to achieve if they know of their own worth and their own individual uniqueness.

When you develop your own self belief, your own uniqueness you will be better prepared to achieve your own greatness, which greatness may be in the public light or it may be within your own family and your own circle of influence. Wherever it is, you will shine and lead and be a strength to others when you decide for yourself that you have the ability to believe in yourself.

Imagine if you will a road, it is a road with many twists and turns and you are walking down this road, you are not alone; in fact, other people on every side of you hem you in. You try to move one way but are pressed back by the people around you; everyday you are on this road not able to move in any direction apart from the one the crowd of people around you are walking in.

Over to the left you catch a glimpse of a brighter place and you wonder what it is, you try to move toward it but the press of the people pushes you back. You keep getting these glimpses of this brighter place and you really want to see what it is and so you push a little harder and for a little longer until finally after many attempts you manage to break through the crowd and get off the road.

You can see the brighter place in front of you but you still need to keep going until you reach it, when you do reach it you find it is the most beautiful place; it gives you a sense of fulfilment, of pleasure and achievement. This place is the real you, it is your destiny, the place that you have worked hard to get to and in time you will see in the distance more brighter places that you will want to work your way towards.

The road you were travelling on was Mediocrity Road, it is the road that the masses of humanity are travelling on and they do not want you to get off of it because that will make them feel that they should do something and that will make them feel uncomfortable. That is why it was difficult to push through the crowd and to get off the road, the fact that you did it shows the belief you have in yourself and your ability to achieve your own destiny.

The greatest blessing you as a mother can give your child is to fight your way off Mediocrity Road, to create your own life and develop your own abilities. As you do your child will see your example and will find their own strength of character and will develop their abilities and achieve their desires and destiny. What a responsibility you have to your child, when you say you want more for your child than you had, it is up to you to do it for yourself and to show them the way.

If you want a good, honest child who is happy and has stability in their life then you will need to be honest, happy and stable in your life. Every time you acknowledge your inability to change and to be what you want to be you are showing your child by example that they cannot change and they cannot be what they want to be. You will find the odd child here and there who will get up and defy their upbringing by becoming successful, some are lucky to find good role models in others, and some are lucky enough to be inspired by a teacher or someone else. Children need examples to follow; role models who will help them to grow and their greatest role model can be you their mother.

You may be asking now how can I develop the self belief that will enable me to reach my potential and develop my life in the way I desire it to be?

Henry Ford said:

"Whether you think you can or think you can't, you're usually right."

Self-Belief is a feeling of being good enough; it's a healthy appreciation of your talents, characteristics and abilities. It's seeing you as special and unique, like no other person on the planet. It is your greatest asset and it will help you to handle whatever life throws at you, it will help you to dig deep into yourself and to rise to any challenge. When you believe in yourself you can be more optimistic, more enthusiastic about everything, you will feel that there is nothing that you couldn't be, do or have in your life.

Confidence plays a big part in self-belief, to be confident is to have faith in yourself and in your ability to do, be, or have whatever you desire. With enough confidence you can do anything, so where do you get that confidence? Well to start with you may at first have to con or trick yourself into having the confidence in yourself to go out into the world and get what you want, simply by putting yourself out there and doing whatever it takes.

Putting on a confident front is easier when you believe in yourself and in whatever you are trying to achieve. If you want to achieve something you will need to believe you can achieve it, you can do this by seeing yourself with your own imagination actually achieving it. You can talk to yourself in a positive way telling yourself that you are good enough and that you can achieve whatever it is you desire. Think of someone you know who is confident and self-assured, they seem to attract others to him or her, they're magnetic and they are more energetic, more uplifting and more optimistic.

Many times you may sabotage yourself by the things you say to yourself and the pictures you let come into your mind. Watch your thoughts and your words because they will build you but they can also destroy you and any efforts you are making to achieve. Following are some things you can do to strengthen your own self-belief.

Be Good to Yourself

It isn't easy to say good things to yourself and to build yourself up. Many of you will feel you are being immodest or arrogant. What you are being is positive and building the good parts of you. When you become aware of the relationship between your thoughts and your behaviour you will realise that saying good things and recognising the good in you is helping you to become the person you really want to be. Tell yourself you are good enough, you are talented and special; you will behave in a way that fulfils the belief. Your belief in yourself and your abilities will make a positive difference in your life and your children's lives.

Keep Moving Forward

When you are living your life in a positive way you will be striving to achieve new levels of living. During this time you will encounter setbacks and challenges that will take all your self-belief and confidence to overcome. Your strong level of self-belief means that whatever you encounter, whatever your experience you will have the internal resources to deal with it and to recover from it.

Your positive self-belief will allow you to stand taller and with greater confidence as you learn from your experience. You can decide now that you will have the strong self-belief that will give you the ability to achieve a greater level of achievement. Again watch your thoughts and your words especially when you hit a setback, take time to recover your confidence and set out again with the new knowledge you have gained from the setback.

Do not let a setback happen without learning something from it, even if it is that you have the resilience and persistence to get back up, dust yourself off and get back on the road again to your achievement.

Respect Yourself

Remember what Marianne Williamson said in her quote:
"We ask ourselves: Who am I to be brilliant, gorgeous, talented, fabulous? Actually who are you not to be?"

When you respect yourself and acknowledge that you are someone and you do have a part to play then you give yourself the power to do, be, or have whatever you want.

Have milestones in your journey to achievement and when you reach a milestone celebrate, do something to show appreciation to yourself for all the effort you have put in to getting to the place you are at. Know for yourself that you are somebody and that you are achieving each and every day.

Be Optimistic

Look around you every so often and notice other people, what do you see in their faces, can you see optimism or pessimism, are they on a road to somewhere or to nowhere, hemmed in by circumstances and other people. These are the two general types of people you will see. They will be in varying degrees of optimism or pessimism but they will fall into these two types. The one with the defeated look where life has taken its toll and they are sinking under the weight of it all and it is showing in their face. Then there is the type that is undefeated, they look fresh and they keep themselves light and cheerful. They have had their challenges but the way they have handled them has made the difference. Their outlook on life is one of optimism and cheerfulness, they are going to keep on, to keep trying and succeeding because they have a self belief that is strong and it gives them the confidence and strength to achieve anything they set their minds to.

You need to be clear about the level of your self-belief now, so you can know what you want to work on in building a stronger self-belief. Think about the different areas of your life and your level of self-belief in each one of them. Your role as a mother maybe one area that you can look at, what is your level of self belief in it, if you gave yourself a mark out of 10 what would it be.

Some other areas you may want to examine could be:

Education   Relationships   Personal Life   Health   Finance

Because this book is about mothering and building your self-belief as a mother I would like you to look at yourself in this area and examine yourself and your ability to be the best mother. What do you feel is your current level of self-belief in your mothering? Now do the following exercise and write out the answers so you can feel and be in touch with yourself on this.

What is my lack of self-belief in my mothering costing me?

Make a list of all the things that this lack of self-belief is costing you, it is important that you grasp the damage that low self belief has done to your life so far.

Now write down what difference it would it make to my life if I doubled my self-belief in my mothering?

Take the time to think about this and allow yourself to get excited at the prospect of leaving behind some of the self limiting beliefs that you have grown out of. Live one day at a time as if you really did have double the amount of self-belief. Every morning choose to be the person who has strong self-belief, ask yourself: What would change? How would I look? Would I be more relaxed, more friendly and happy?

Make a list of a few things that you might do when having a strong self-belief that you didn't do before.

You may want to study some other people who have high self-belief, look at what they do and how they act? Ensure that the people you study do have high self-belief, just because people are famous and successful does not always mean they have high self-belief, in fact some celebrities do not cope well with being famous because their self-belief is not strong. Many turn to drugs or other vices to help them have the strength to cope with the pressure of fame whereas if they developed a great self-belief they would have the ability to cope.

As a mother who has great self-belief you will be a good role model for your child and they will not need to look at celebrities or any one else to feel good about themselves. You will give them everything they need to develop their own life and success in their own world.

Your expectations of yourself will be the key to your achieving whatever you set out to achieve, expect great things of yourself and then walk the path to your destiny knowing that with your strong self-belief you can go to wherever you choose. Also let your child know of what you expect of them, let them feel how great you think they are by expecting them to be great and they will rise to whatever you expect of them

Chapter Four

∞

VISUALISE YOUR FUTURE

T HE ability to visualise is the ability to see where you are going, to actually picture in your mind the outcome you desire. Your mind is very powerful, far more powerful than anything else on this earth and visualisation is one of the most powerful tools of the mind. The masses of people will say they believe when they can see what they want in front of them or seeing is believing, they want the evidence before they will commit themselves to believing.

People who are using their mind effectively will know and say that if they believe first, if they can see the picture in their mind first then their belief can bring about the situation they desire. This is believing then seeing and it works through the law of cause and effect or the law of attraction which is one and the same. If you can visualise an outcome that you desire and hold a strong picture of it in your mind, then you will actually take the actions required to bring about that outcome in a way that is remarkable.

This is the way things were created and out of all the living things upon this planet human beings are the only ones given the ability to imagine, to be able to see in their minds eye something they desire or even don't desire. This gift or mind tool is one of the greatest in your effort to create your future, the future you desire that will bring you happiness, joy and peace of mind.

The ability to visualise is very important to you but many of you do not use it effectively or even use it at all. One reason for this is that you were probably told as a child to stop day dreaming or to be real about life, to get caught up in dreams would not get us anywhere and you needed to accept who you are and to get on with whatever you were born with.

I ask the question, why would you be given the ability to do some-thing if you were not allowed to use it for your own benefit and the benefit of those around you? Think now of the inventors, the artists, the dreamers who have given so much of their mind and ability so that the world today can have all the modern conveniences that make light work of living. The car, washing machine, vacuum cleaner, electricity, light bulb, great works of art, and many, many other inventions.

Are you grateful to Thomas Edison who used his imagination to bring light into the home, I am sure you have experienced a power cut even if only for a few minutes, if it is at night then I know you can ap-preciate how dark it gets when there is no light at all. I am not sure what inspired Edison to work upon this project but I know he would never have done it without his ability to visualise what he wanted to achieve and to continue to visualise his way to a successful outcome.

It was not an easy task, it took great thought and thousands of at-tempts to get a working model of what he visualised in the first place. One of the biggest challenges today for each of you is to be able to see past what you already have in your life and to visualise something greater. As a mother you have the greatest opportunity to create life and then to use your imagination and visualise what future you would like for that life you have created.

Think back to the birth of your first child, what were some of the thoughts in your mind, what pictures did you conjure up in your mind about this child? You probably had pictures of a happy baby, and happy toddler and a wonderful child who loved life and achievement. I am sure none of you imagined anything negative for this child you were creating within you and that you wanted the very best for them.

This is visualising, it is using your own creative mind power to cre-ate the life you want for you and for your child. It is one of the most effective tools you have within you for the development and creation of your future. When you use it effectively and are focused upon a posi-tive outcome it will help you to have all you desire, when used to focus upon a negative outcome it is just as powerful in bringing you all that you do not want.

Pictures can be very powerful, I am sure you have had strong emo-tions roused by the pictures you see on TV, maybe of a natural disas-ter that has happened and the pictures coming through the TV are stirring something inside of you that is moving you emotionally and creating within you thoughts and feelings that reach out to the people suffering in this disaster. Visualisation works in much the same way, the pictures you create in your own mind can stir up feelings and move you emotionally to create more pictures and more feelings upon which you will act and which will provide results in your life which in turn will become your circumstances.

Come with me now and try this little exercise in using your imagination, think of a past experience, one that was very enjoyable and that made you very happy. It may have been something that happened on holiday or anywhere, just make sure it was a good experience and you had strong feelings of joy and happiness from it. If you cannot think of an actual experience then make one up, think of something you would like to have happen.

Now you have the experience in your mind I would like you to make it more enjoyable, add more colour to the picture, more noise and make it bigger, bring it closer to you if you want to. Are you in the picture or are you looking at it from the outside? All these questions will help you to create a picture within your own mind, do not be concerned that it is not real or that you cannot actually see the picture, some people may see images others may just feel the images within them.

What is this past experience that you are visualising like for you; can you feel the happiness and excitement that were there at the actual time of the experience? This is visualising, many of you use it everyday to relive experiences of the past, unfortunately it can be used negatively as well as positively and it can also be a power within you to keep you bound by chains when you keep visualising the negative things in your life, like times when you have been hurt and upset by someone and you keep going over and over visualising each time what happened and how it made you feel. Just like you can build the good experience and let it help you feel good, you can also build up the bad experience and let it help you to feel bad.

Many people do this and they keep themselves tied to experiences that do not lift and inspire them but they bring them down into the depths of misery and the more they visualise them and add more and more emotion to them they are tied tighter and tighter with negative chains that limit them and their thinking until their ability to visualise a good future is gone. Fortunately your ability to visualise never disappears it is only your motive for doing it that gets shrouded by other things, you get distracted by other things that are happening around you and you forget to use the brilliant tools of the mind that are yours and that can help you to build your life in a way that will benefit you, your child and your community.

Go back to your good experience and see how easy it is to use your past good experiences to create a future you can enjoy and continue to build upon. Might I suggest also that you can use your power of visualisation to let go of some of the past experiences that are limiting you and that you are carrying around with you as a packhorse would carry its burden. Lighten your own load and see how much more enjoyable life can be when you are not burdened with experiences that do not serve you. You can do this by visualising all the negative and heavy things you are carrying just falling away from you, they are falling into space behind you and they disappear, you cannot see where they have gone and there is no way to get them back, they are gone forever. Visualising this can be powerful in helping you to let go of things that are holding you down, that are weighing you down to the point of not being able to move forward and progress.

Take the time to experiment with this letting go process, imagine yourself walking down the road and as you do all the negative hurts and the heavy sorrows are falling away from you, they are falling behind you and then disappearing. Actually visualise this happening within you, have a focused picture in your mind of your burdens just dropping from your shoulders and behind you into non existence, can you feel how much lighter you feel? Remember a lot of the burdens you are carrying are only in your mind, they are past hurts and experiences that you have accepted into your life through someone else's opinion of a situation or someone else's actions and choices. It maybe that you are carrying burdens that you have taken upon yourself through your misinterpretation of an event or experience. If you want to go forward in your life you will need to let go of these burdens, they are clouding your mind to the extent that you cannot see clearly to move forward and progress.

Keep doing this exercise until you really feel you are free from past hurts and negative experiences, how does this feel? When you feel you have truly let go you will feel a freedom, a space in your life to fill with experiences that build you and help you to feel good. Now that space needs to be filled with good and pleasurable experiences and this is

were you can use visualisation to imagine what you would like to fill
your life with. You are creating your future; make sure it is what you
want. As a mother I am sure it will involve your child and how you,
as this empowered and enlightened person can help them to use their
own powers of visualisation to create their own future.

You know how powerful visualisation is if you have done the exercise, use this power daily to create the experiences you want. Teach your
child how to use this power in its own life and let them feel the power
that is in them to create the future they desire. You could play games
in getting them to imagine something, to see it in their mind and then
to draw it on paper. I am sure your child may do this already, especially
if they are younger, it is sometimes with older children and teenagers
that you may find they are not using their imaginations as they could,
this may be because of their own past experiences. Find opportunities
to get them to experiment with this, it can give great enjoyment, touch
the emotions and empower them to feel good about life.

As a mother you have the greatest opportunity to affect your child's
life for good or for bad, it is your choice, you have within you the greatest tools to help you to be the greatest mother and woman there is.
When you learn about these tools and how to use them then you can
be effective in directing your own life and also the life of your child. Do
not be afraid to guide and direct your child, they need it, they want you
to help them to know which direction they should go.

Use your imagination once more and come on a journey with me,
you are your child and you are going to live in their shoes for a few
minutes. They are in school, you as a mother are not there to protect
them or to guide them, they are on their own, a friend wants them to
do something and they know they should not do it. They have to make
a decision here and that decision will take them one way or another,
they could decide to go ahead and do whatever it is and keep their
friend and also get the power that comes from their bravado or they
choose to refuse to do it and risk feeling the derision that may come
from them choosing to follow the values you have given them, to know
right from wrong and to choose to do the right.

Visualise the situation and see your child in this dilemma, how does
it feel? What do you do? Children go through these experiences on a
daily basis, you as a mother can help them to cope with them by helping them to create a strength within them that will let them know that

no matter what others may think and say, they will walk their own path through life and be stronger for it. If you as a mother can teach your child and let them know what to do in such situations, and help them to feel the benefit of making the right decision, you will build within them a resilience that will serve them all their lives.

It is a child's lack of values and direction that causes them to feel the pressure to conform to what other children around them are doing and urging them to do. Lift your child's vision to a higher and greater level, help them to see further than the situation in front of them and they will know what to do and will be far happier in their life because of the vision you have given them. Think about this for yourself, look at how much easier you find life when you know where you are going and why you are going there. It is the same for everyone even your child, they need the solid foundation of knowing who they are and what they are and they can get this from using the power of visualisation in their lives.

You can use visualisation to see how good a community can be when the people have solid values; it gives direction and people know who they are and why they are. You can start with yourself and use your own power of visualisation to create your future and then when you are doing it for yourself you can do it for your child and then you can help your friends and your child can help their friends and very soon you can have a community that is pleasant and pleasurable.

My daughter had this experience when she was in school. It had been reported to the school that two young girls had been seen taking flowers from the graves in the church graveyard. There was no description of the girls and the head teacher had asked for them to own up. My daughter knew it was her two friends because they had told her and having the value of honesty in her life she managed to talk her friends into going to the head teacher and accept responsibility for their actions. This saved the whole school being punished and under condemnation and it helped the young girls to feel better that they did not have this matter hanging over their heads.

If you want to live a life of peace and happiness, to be able to feel good even when things are not so good then use the power of your own mind, visualise how you want things to be and know that everything you need is within you and you can use it freely, it costs nothing but some concentration, some self-belief and effort. Let your light shine, feel your own power and create the life you want to live, let go of anything that is holding you back, whether it is anger, jealousy, pride or any other burden, just let it go and put something good in the place of it.

Your life is an open book and you write the pages each day, turn over the page and start writing a brand new chapter, don't worry about mistakes, learn from them and erase them by making greater effort to be the person you want to be. Remember to use the power of your own visualisation to decide the life you would like to create for yourself and also for your child, remember you are their role model, their example, whatever you want for your child you can give them through your own thoughts and actions.

Take time now to answer the following questions, write down as much as you like, be as detailed as you can:

What do I really want my life to be?

Why do I really want it to be that way?

Chapter Five

∽

AFFIRM YOUR SUCCESS

You are remarkable; you have been given some remarkable gifts that will help you to travel the road you choose to travel through life. They will help you to have, do or be whatever you chose in your life, it is your choice as to whether you use these gifts or whether you leave them dormant within you, never to feel the exhilaration of living your life with vision and direction. Your success in any endeavour will come as you develop habits that assist you to think the thoughts that will give you the emotional support to take the action you desire. Your thoughts, emotions and acts will determine your success; an example of this would be as follows:

It is your greatest desire to be successful in learning to drive a car, your first knowledge of this desire will come from your thoughts, it could be that you are a passenger in a car when **thoughts** come to you about how you would find life so much easier if you could drive yourself. You nurture these thoughts until you begin to **feel** (emotion) some enthusiasm for having the ability to drive, this **feeling** grows until you find the **opportunity** (action) to put your **thoughts** and **feelings** into **action**.

Can you see now how everything falls into place, first a thought, then a feeling and then you take the necessary action to bring about whatever it is you desire to achieve. One of the ways you can ensure your success in any venture is by auto-suggestion: this is, as the word suggests that you suggest to yourself the things that you desire and you continue to suggest it until you have achieved it.

The suggestion to your mind of something you would like to achieve is only half of what you need, the other half comes from the way you talk to yourself. Your self-talk, you may think that you do not talk to yourself and you may not out loud where you can see, feel and hear yourself, but inside you are talking to yourself all the time. Listen to yourself now, you are either thinking 'yes I do talk to myself all the time' or you are thinking this woman is mad to think that I talk to myself.

Whatever it is that you say and the words you use are your self-talk, even though the words are in your head and you do not utter them they are still having some affect upon you and your life. Let's look at an example – over the last couple of years you have put on a little weight, it has crept on slowly and you have managed not to get to concerned about it until you get out a dress you would like to wear for a party. You try the dress on and it does not fit, you are now saying to yourself, 'why did I let myself get so fat.' or something similar to that.

What your self-talk is suggesting to you now is that you are fat and the very words you use will trigger thoughts, feelings and actions to up-hold your words. If you continue to use these words they will become a habit and will become part of a cycle of thoughts, feelings and actions that will confirm your words about you being fat.

Let us follow through on this example and say you come to a point in your life where you desire to stop being fat and to become slim, fit and healthy. This new desire could have come about from some outside force or from within you, which ever it is you can use it to help you to start a new line of self-talk that will suggest to you that you are slim, fit and healthy.

You are now on the threshold of doing something that will take effort and will power and you will need to find ways in which you can have this will power in your life constantly to help you to fight the affects of your deeply ingrained habits. One way of doing this is to start affirming the new behaviour and results you want in your life.

What does it mean to affirm something?

When you affirm that you will be slim, fit and healthy you are saying 'I can be slim, fit and healthy' or you are saying 'I can't be slim, fit and healthy.' Both are affirming something you are going to become or not become. The difference between 'I can' or 'I can't' will be the difference in the action you take and the results you achieve.

Experiment with the words, say 'I can' how does that feel, can you feel any emotion within you. If not then say it again with a little more strength behind the words. Say it until you can feel the enthusiasm and excitement for the thing that you can do, be, or have. This is affirming your desire to yourself through the action of auto-suggestion, and you can use this auto-suggestion to change anything you desire to change in your life by writing out short phrases written in the positive that you can repeat to yourself daily, affirming to your mind that this is your desire and you wish to achieve this change.

Now you understand auto-suggestion you can start to change your life in whatever way you desire by having some affirmations that will focus your thoughts and feelings upon a desired achievement, such as, I am slim, fit and healthy and weigh …? Whatever it is you desire to weigh.

When I was younger there was an advert that came on the television and the jingle said:

"A hundred housewives everyday pick up a tin of beans and say 'Beans means Heinz."

These words written to a catchy tune have stuck in my mind for the past 20 or so years, how powerful are the words we use when we use them well, this advert was so expertly written and delivered that I would not buy any other brand of beans except Heinz even today.

This example shows you how you can use the power of words to achieve or change anything you want to in your life. By affirming your desires on a regular basis just like the advertisers do, you are programming your mind to achieve that desire. An affirmation is a short phrase written in a positive way and is affirming something you want.

Notice the words you say to yourself now and see if they are giving you the results you want; let us look at the area of Health in your life. You are feeling tired most of the time and do not have the energy to keep going and therefore you feel lethargic and depressed because you can see the results you want in life slipping away. What are the words you are saying, they maybe things like 'I am fat'. 'I am tired', 'I am no good', 'I can't do anything', and probably many other similar phrases which when said over and over again even quietly in your head will have the affect of making you feel lethargic, tired and depressed.

You can change this downward spiral in your life by changing the words you speak, by saying 'I am slim, fit and healthy' you can change the way you feel about yourself and your life, and the words themselves suggest energy and enthusiasm. You may say that it is not true, you are not slim, fit and healthy and therefore you would be lying to yourself.

An affirmation can be a statement of something you want and you are affirming to achieve it. It may not be true now but you are not affirming what you are now, you are changing the self talk you have been using for affirmations that you want to achieve in the future and therefore they are true it is just that they are a little way down the road and you are affirming yourself toward them.

You are not trying to convince anyone else but yourself about your new desire, you are not misguiding anyone else not even yourself, what you are doing is using positive self-talk to achieve a desire. Affirming your success can be used in any area of your life, it doesn't matter what it is you can find a positive affirmation to achieve your desires. It could be financial, educational, health, relationships, social or spiritual or your career.

As a mother you have the greatest career there is, you are in the most important sector of people in the country because if you did not choose that career and if everyone decided against the career of motherhood within 50 years the race would have died out, there would be very few people left and there would be no one left who could take on the career of motherhood. So you are vital to the building of the country and especially to the economic growth of the country because you are providing tomorrow's leaders, inventors, entrepreneurs and workers. You are not only giving birth to them you are also training and developing them to become who they need to be to continue the way of life as we know it.

How effective a mother do you think you will be if you are affirming to yourself regularly the 'I am not good enough' 'I can't do this or that' 'I don't count', if you listen to yourself and what you are saying quietly in your head you will be able to see why you think, feel and act as you do. If your circumstances are that there is never enough money to go around you will find yourself affirming that there is never enough and this will affect your children, even if you do not say it in those words your child will pick up on your thoughts and feelings from your behaviour toward yourself and them.

As this book is about mothering you can look at how using positive affirmation can help you to become a great mother and they can help your child become a great person. A good positive affirmation could be 'I am a good mother' this is short, positive and inspires you to become a good mother. It is general but will still guide you in your thoughts about mothering and it will inspire you in what you would like to achieve as a good mother.

Imagine your fairy godmother has appeared and has waved her magic wand over you, she has given you all the characteristics you desire to become the good mother you want to be. Notice that I said 'good' here and not perfect, do not weigh yourself down with the thoughts and pictures of being the perfect mother, do your best and keep doing your best and each day you will improve and succeed in being the mother you desire to be. Do not look to be perfect, look for happiness in what you are doing and achieving, and this will make life better for everyone.

Now in your imagination you can see what can be yours because the Fairy Godmother just gave it to you. Keep that picture firmly in your mind and now come back to the present and use your picture of your desire to write some affirmations. For instance if the picture in your imagination showed you playing and teaching your child you could affirm:

"'I am a good mother and I teach my child through play.'

This is affirming that you are a good mother and it is also saying that you will play with your child and use that play to teach them things.

Think about when you are out with your child and you are crossing roads, you do not go out especially to learn how to cross the road; you do it all the time when you are out anywhere. If you come to a road you teach the child to look right then left and then right again before crossing it. You are teaching them about cars and speed, you are helping them to learn through their everyday activities.

When you use affirmation you are developing habits, your life is made up of your habits, the things you do on a daily basis without even thinking you are doing them. A habit is formed by repetition of doing something over and over again until it becomes automatic. Our habits are not just physical but they are mental too and what affirmation is doing is developing new mental habits to replace the old self-limiting habits.

Think about what you want to achieve as a mother, look again at the picture you created when the fairy Godmother waved her wand, which could be a good place to start to achieve your desires. Of course another way of finding what you want is to visualise as we discussed in the last chapter. See what you desire, feel it, hear it, smell it and touch it; use all your senses to create the picture of what you desire. You have five senses in which you learn everything in your world and affirmation is using your sense of hearing.

When you know what you want to achieve, write it down and then decide why you want to achieve it, the reason you look at why is because it will take great effort to change your thinking and develop new habits. If you have a strong enough 'why' it will help you to get through some of the tough times. Once you know why you want it, now decide when you want it and set yourself a time frame. This will have the effect of keeping you focused on becoming whatever it is you have decided to become. Also make sure that what you have desired is attainable and realistic for you. It would be difficult to become an airhostess if you have a small child depending on you being around everyday. You can also make it measurable by breaking it down into smaller segments so you can see small achievements along the way and this will act as a motivator.

Now you have the steps to forming new habits through affirmation how is this going to affect your children? It will affect them greatly as you develop your mothering ability and that will give them more positive experiences in their childhood which in turn will affect their choices in life as they grow older. They also will learn to use affirmation and goal setting in their lives to achieve much greater results than they would have without the positive role model you have been to them.

As you grow and as you develop your abilities your children will learn from them. They will grow and develop in much the same way. A child is in close proximity to you most of the time especially for the first four or five years, it is your privilege to be able to mould that child, to help develop the characteristics that will make them who they are as adults. This is why mothers are the most important people in the country; they are essential to the success of the home, of the community and of the country.

Start now to affirm your own importance so that you can be successful as a mother and as a person, so you can make a difference to your family and to your community. It does not matter whether you are a two parent family, a single mother or whatever your circumstances, stand up and be counted, start to recognise and build your own abilities so that you are effective in your child's life and in turn your child is effective in his or her own life. As was said during the wars, 'your country needs you'. You are valuable and you need to recognise this in what you say to yourself each and everyday.

Chapter Six

꩜

THE POWER OF HABIT

H ABIT is formed through repetition, if you think of a piece of thread wrapped around your wrist, on its own it is easily breakable, you could pull it and it would break but then wrap it around twice and you may still be able to break it but it would be a little harder to do. Wrap it again and again and with each strand it will become harder and harder to break. This is like habits the more you repeat them the harder it becomes to break the cycle. A habit is something that you do automatically, something that through constant repetition has become an automatic response. An example of this could be driving a car, when you first get into a car and learn to drive it you have to think of everything you need to do and do them one at a time. After a while of practising and working toward learning all the steps you need to take to get the car moving in the direction you desire to go, these steps start to become automatic. That means when you get into the car you do not have to sit there and say 'mirror, signal, manoeuvre', this becomes automatic. You do not have to think about changing the gear at a certain speed or sound, it becomes automatic. This is the power of habit, practised and developed over time and with effort.

Many times you may want something and start to work to develop your ability to be, do or have that thing but because it does not happen as quick and easily as you desire you give up before it becomes a habit thereby missing out on what could have been if you had persevered long enough for it to become habitual in your life. The power of habit is a good power as well as a bad power depending upon which habit you are developing.

Think of some of your habits now and decide if they are good or bad ones. You may have the habit of eating healthy food and exercising on a regular basis to keep your body and your mind focused and responsive, this would be a good habit. You could have the opposite of eating unhealthy foods and taking no exercise and your mind would be fuddled and unresponsive. The choice is yours as to which habit you develop but the consequences, the responsive or unresponsive mind and body are consequential upon the actions you take and the habit you develop in your life.

So, why do you do the things you do when you know the things you know?

Many times you do what comes naturally and easily, it is easy to eat what you want, when you want it. Your body will crave things that are pleasurable and easily available such as sugar, fats and processed foods. Not only do they taste nice, they are also easy to get and do not require a lot of work and attention to acquire. Your thoughts very quickly pick up on the pleasure and ease of having these foods and very soon it can become habitual to eat them.

Your habits are formed not just from the eating action but also from the thoughts and feelings you receive while eating the foods. Think about a bar of chocolate and the pleasure you receive from it. Imagine now eating a bar of chocolate. First you desired to eat the chocolate, you remembered the pleasure you got from eating it and this feeling makes your need to eat the chocolate so much stronger. Then you find yourself craving the chocolate and then the physical act of eating it fulfils the need, which then instils the habit a little stronger within you.

Habits are made in every area of your life, in relationships you can get into habits of how you treat people or respond to certain situations. If a person says something to you in a certain tone you can respond to that tone, if it is high pitched you may respond in a way that is angry or frustrated. If it is low pitched you may respond in a manner that is gentle and loving. It depends upon the habits you have developed toward the person speaking and what they say and how they say it. You can have different responses to different people depending upon the relationship you have with them and the habit you have developed about them.

In finances you may have habits developed from childhood that will either keep you financially broke or financially free. In education you may have the habit of thinking you cannot 'do numbers' and never succeed at it simply because you have a habit of thinking you cannot do it. Perhaps because some one told you when you were younger that you could not 'do numbers' you therefore you developed the habit of thinking and feeling you could not do it.

No habit is unbreakable.

It will take great effort and focus to break a habit that does not serve you but it can be broken and disappear from your life if you are willing to do what it takes. It requires a willing mind and another habit to replace it with. If you want to change the habit of eating unhealthy food you will need to replace that habit with eating healthy food. You cannot get rid of one habit without replacing it with something else or you leave a void that will be filled with maybe another bad habit.

If you are going to change a bad habit have a good one to put in its place. An example of this is when people decide to change the habit of smoking. They do not just stop smoking they also replace it with an alternative. Some people will eat a sweet or chew something; others will do something to help them deny the craving for a cigarette. It is wise to be careful what you replace the habit with; you don't want to replace a bad habit with another bad habit.

The power of thought can be very helpful in changing habits that hold you bound. Every time a bad habit rears its head you can be ready with thoughts that will help you overcome it. You can have affirmations that you can say quietly to yourself or out loud, it is up to you! An affirmation can help you through by focusing your thoughts upon what you want. If you are giving up eating foods that are bad for you then you may have an affirmation that says something like: 'I am slim, fit and healthy and I weigh…?'

This will help you to overcome the craving for the food that is not healthy and does not keep you slim or fit. It will require great effort at first to ignore the cravings for the unhealthy food which is bad for you but the more you succeed in not eating it, the easier it becomes. Think of the thread of habit making again, breaking the habit is very much like unwrapping each layer of thread and with each successful effort you make, it is one less thread to break and it becomes easier to break. Remember each time you choose to unwind that thread you are winding another healthier thread and making a healthy habit that will be good for you.

Habits are breakable; they just take effort and time to do it. As a mother you will be developing habits within yourself and your child and one of the first of these will be a sleeping habit or pattern. A habit is a pattern of behaviour that you follow in a certain thing. A child very quickly and astutely develops habits that will suit them and give them what they want. In sleeping for instance, a baby will like sleeping next to the mother, this is because they can feel the mother and hear her breathing and they feel comfortable and secure there.

That may not be good for the baby nor is it good for you. The mother who will not get the sleep she needs. The baby may need to be close enough to you to be aware of your presence but it does not need to be right next to you. This will build a habit of dependence that would, as the child gets older, prove to be something that could hold the child bound. If the child feels secure and happy that you are there and available when needed, the child will develop a pattern of independence that will help as it gets older, to grow and develop skills and behaviour that give confidence.

As a mother there are many habits you will develop in your life with the child and also in the work it takes to raise the child. These habits will be good and bad ones and you will need to look at your habits and decide which ones are serving you and which ones are limiting you. I had six children in thirteen years and that meant I had eight people all wearing different clothes everyday so I developed the habit of washing and ironing at certain times in a manner that took the least effort so as I could keep up with the work load. This became very important to me and even today when my children are gone and doing their own washing, I still have the habit of ensuring my washing is done quickly and with the least effort.

Another habit I decided I needed to break was one of shouting and disciplining my children in a way that was not working. I would get angry and shout at them and smack them, but all that was achieving was allowing me to vent my frustration in a way that said to my children I did not love them. I remember saying to my friend that I was not going to do that anymore and worked out how I was going to achieve it. I decided on other ways of dealing with the situations that would arise and then when something did happen I could deal with it in a reasonable manner. I do remember after achieving this, my daughter said to me that she was pleased I did not shout and smack her any more. This gave me more impetus to go forward with my new behaviour and also developed greater peace and harmony in the home.

One of the ways I dealt with my frustration or anger was to move out of the room if I could feel myself getting irritated or angry. Another was to distract the child from whatever they where doing. As they got older I tried hard to remember that some of their behaviour was about them trying out and pushing for bigger boundaries. There is usually a reason why a child is acting out, it is important to remember that children have feelings and emotions and they can feel frustration too.

If you are like most people you will wish you were more disciplined in your habits and you may find yourself wishing you could change some of them. However you may find yourself procrastinating this desire as it requires too much effort thereby never changing. In today's world we are used to getting everything instantly, like picking up the telephone and being able to talk to a person instantly even if they are half way across the world. Being able to open a can and eat the food you desire almost instantly. We are so used to getting what we want instantly that if it takes some time we become impatient and tend to give up.

Changing habits takes discipline, it takes time and you will need to delay your gratification, which is receiving instant results, until you have invested enough time and effort to gain such results. In the instant world you are used to this will not be easy but it is possible it just takes patience and discipline. My definition of Discipline is this:

'A disciple is a follower, someone who follows a leader, like Jesus Christ had disciples who followed Him. Disciple is the first half of the word and line is the second half, so discipline is to follow the line.'

If you want to achieve something you can draw a line between where you are now and were you want to be. To achieve this you simply stick to the line you have drawn. That line will represent the behaviour you will cultivate to achieve your desire. So for instance if you want to change the habit of not exercising to exercising regularly you will decide what you want to achieve, how much and what exercise you will do and then have a plan to achieve that exercise. The plan will be the line that you follow, such as each morning I will walk two miles in 30 minutes and in the evening I will complete 10 minutes exercise to tone muscle. This routine should be the line you follow everyday.

Discipline will make life much easier and is well worth developing in your life. Think of a habit you would like to change in your life, now ask yourself why you want to change that habit. Knowing why you want something is important because when it gets hard and you really need to be disciplined knowing why you are doing it will help you. Now you know the habit and why you want to change it make a plan on how you are going to change it. This plan is the line you are going to follow each and every day. It is what will help you to be disciplined and to achieve your goal. Do not worry if you wander from the line a little, the important bit will be that you stay as close as you can to the line, always coming back to it if you wander off.

Now mark 21 days on your calendar, this is how long you are giving yourself to overcome a habit, this means for the next 21 days you are going to give yourself over to breaking a habit or developing a new good habit. Now you also have a time limit to work toward it should give·you more impetus and confidence to get going and to achieve. Remember the why in what you are doing, particularly when things get difficult and you just want to give in.

Try to work on one habit at a time, if you have too many habits it will be like trying to catch three balls that are thrown at you simultaneously. They come from different directions and you may miss all three. So work on one habit for 21 days and then it should be fairly well established. Then you can go on to work on the next one for another 21 days. Working in this way you can change or develop 17 habits in one year, think about how you can transform your life one habit at a time.

You can follow this six-step process to break and develop your habits and to have discipline in your life.

STEP ONE:
What Do You Want?

This first step is to identify what it is you want to change. Is it something you do now that you would like to stop doing, or something you would like to accomplish? You can use this step to describe the result you would like to achieve. Write it down so you can read it regularly and find the motivation you need to keep going.

STEP TWO:
Follow a Role Model

Look for someone else who has achieved your desire. Knowing that they have accomplished it will help you to achieve. You do not need to know the achiever personally neither do they have to be living. The point is to think and learn about people who had control in this area and then to emulate them.

STEP THREE:
See Your Success

List the benefits you will acquire becoming disciplined in this area, ask yourself 'How will this make life better for me?' Ask yourself why you want to receive the rewards from changing this habit or developing a new habit, list the rewards and it will help you to be willing to work harder. It will help if you can write in a way that you can actually feel, see, smell, taste and touch how it will be once you are disciplined in this area.

STEP FOUR:
Watch for the danger zones.

You can consider here where you might fall and what could happen that will lead you astray. If you are watching what you eat, it could be that Christmas is coming or there could be situations or people that will cause you a problem in staying disciplined. It maybe that evening times are difficult for you and they will be your danger zones. Plan for these times, list potential danger times or situations that you need to be avoid, if you know in advance then you can be ready for them with a plan on how to handle the situation

STEP FIVE:
Make Decisions in Advance

This means to decide in advance what you are going to do in certain situations. You have heard the saying, 'Say NO to Drugs' This is advance decision making, you are deciding in advance what you will do if someone offers you drugs, you will say 'no'. You can use this step to plan what you will say or do, when situations arise that could keep you from your goal.

STEP SIX:
Have a Support Network

This step is important, it can be the real power behind your changing, and it will help you to change your life. Find someone whom you respect enough to ask them to help you to achieve in whatever area you are trying to change. Many people who are trying to become slim, fit and healthy will join a slimming club and use this as their support. Many other people will have life coaches; you will find having someone to support you, to lift you when you need it will be a real help to you. Your support team will also hold you accountable to achieve what you said you would achieve, this again will help you so much in being disciplined.

As with any habit you are trying to overcome there will always be times when you will weaken and relapse. As you are trying to discipline yourself in new behaviour this will happen and if you are prepared for it you will handle it so much better. Be aware of the things you may say to yourself that will sideline you from your course for good. If you know of them they will be easier to handle. Number one is thinking that once will be enough, having just one cigarette, one drink, letting go with anger one time. Once is never enough and when you have done it once you will do it again. If you are tempted, let the red flag fly and warn you of the danger.

Number two follows on from number one, once you have succumbed you then say to yourself 'Now you have blown it, you might as well mess it up properly and have another and yet another.

Number three then follows from number two where you have given up. You feel terrible because you have faltered and you end up saying something like,' I am hopeless', 'I am worthless,' 'I will never be able to control my habits,' 'I give up.'

Reject all three of these steps, you do not have to give up, you can get back on the discipline line and acknowledge that you just wandered off for a short while but now you are back, stronger and more determined to succeed. You are worth it, you can do it, whatever it is in your life that you want to be more disciplined in, you can do it, you just need to keep going and keep trying.

As a mother your example of discipline will have a great affect on your children, they will be watching and learning all the time. When you understand this you will find it easier because of your love for the child. I remember many years ago my daughter had a friend whose parents smoked quite heavily and they felt tied to this habit. They would tell the daughter that she should never start smoking and warned her how hard it was to stop.

When this girl became 15 she started to smoke, why would she do that if her parents had told her how bad it was and how hard it was to stop? Because the parents' example is far stronger than their words, why would she believe it was bad if they were doing it?

The power of habit is strong; develop habits that will serve you and your family. Remember that the things you say to yourself everyday will have an impact upon you, so say things to yourself that strengthen you and help you to feel good about yourself and your life. As a mother you have the greatest job in the world, the moulding and shaping of the child you love and want the best for, they will follow you wherever you go. Discipline yourself to be the leader your child will try to emulate. Start today to follow through on all the things you want to achieve as a mother.

Do not dwell on what is past, you cannot change that and don't worry about the future that will take care of itself. Focus on today and what you can do today to help yourself and your child to have the greatest life there is. They will thank you for it and will rise up and call your name blessed.

Part Two

∞

HOW THE MIND WORKS

The second part of this book is all about the mind, how it works and how you can reprogramme it to bring you the life you most desire.

Many times you think that there is nothing you can do to change some part of your life, there is always something you can do to change and manage to bring about circumstances that help you to progress and to achieve your desired ends.

Knowing how you mind operates is a great help in this because you can then be aware of the pitfalls and the reasons why your life is the way it is.

I hope you enjoy the information that follows and that you try out the various exercises. It is great fun and very exhilarating to think, feel and act differently and see the results that come from this.

Have the greatest time finding out about how your mind has been programmed and how you can reprogramme it.

Chapter Seven

∽

THE MIND, SPIRIT AND BODY

S IR Winston Churchill said many years ago that one of the greatest
assets of any country was the health of its citizens. It is important
to have a healthy mind as well as a healthy body so, what is a healthy
mind and how does it work?

You probably do not think too much about the mind and how it is
working each and every second of your life. It has such a great affect
upon your life and happiness that it is worth taking a look at, so you
can find the best way to use your mind and get the most out of your
life.

In the world you live in there are six billion minds that is six billion
people all looking at their lives and experiences everyday, every minute
in their own way, seeing things their own way through their own window on life.

This window is a metaphoric window like when people say 'you see
the world through rose tinted glasses,' it is not an actual window. It is
your perspective of life, the way you see and interpret your life in your
world. The problem is that the window they are looking through is
distorted somewhat by the beliefs and experiences they have had in
their own lives. Imagine that you are a brand new baby, just been born,
your window on life is clean and clear, there is no distortion, no dirt or
mess to obscure your view on life. The only thing is you are too young
and helpless to take advantage of this brilliant view of life, and you are
bound to your mother who has her view on life and how it should be.

The problem with this is that your mothers' view is obscured by her
life experiences. She will make decisions and view life through her own
beliefs and experiences and some of those beliefs have come from her

mother. So you can see that from a very early age you will have been given beliefs about life that can hinder and make you afraid of certain things. Of course there is the opposite, which is, you will be given beliefs that will build you and help you to develop into the person you were born to be.

So your beautiful clean window on life may become a little dirty and difficult to see through, how dirty and how difficult depends on your life experience. The amazing thing about it is that once you understand the concept of the window, you can choose to clean your window and to change some of the conditioning and beliefs that have been put there. That is when you can decide for yourself what beliefs you want and which ones are limiting you and you want to dispose of.

Your mind is versatile; it is possible to change it, to reprogramme what has been put there by yourself and others, to clean your metaphoric window and to see life differently. This is essential if you are to change anything about your life; it first has to change within you before you can change any outside circumstance.

The circumstances you have in your life come from the thoughts, feelings and actions you have experienced in your life so far. If you are to change any circumstance you disapprove of, this will require you to change your view on that particular trait. This means cleaning your window of that circumstance or to change the way you view it and believe it to be.

To do this you need to know how your mind is made up and how it takes in information and uses it. How your mind is constructed and what it looks like. Your mind is the most sophisticated and complex instrument on the planet and very few people have any idea of what the mind is actually like, how to describe it and how to change it forever. You will say you have to change your mind but until you know what it looks like and how it works you are stuck with what you have in life.

You take information into your mind everyday through your five senses, what you see, hear, touch, smell or taste. This is the way you learn and develop your thoughts; the following diagram will help you to understand what happens to the information when it enters the mind.

When the information goes into your mind it hits three filters, one is delete, you can see, hear, touch, smell and taste tens of thousands of different bits of information in a day. If your mind did not delete some of this information it would not be able to cope with it. If you think about your left foot now, you will probably know what it feels like but before it being mentioned your mind was deleting what it felt like because it did not need to know. If you get a pain in your left foot then your mind will think about it because the pain will alert it.

You can also use the delete filter to delete information you do not want to take into your mind, such as if someone says something you do not want to hear or you do not need you can delete it and not let it take root in your mind. The same with the other senses, you can choose to accept or reject anything by using the delete filter.

The next filter is the distortion filter, this is the filter that you use to take the information coming in through your senses and you distort it to fit your values and beliefs. This is where you can get a lot of misunderstandings and upsets because you are distorting what someone is saying or doing to fit what you believe.

Example: someone says to you "You look very nice and slim in that dress" you hear and think 'don't I usually look nice and slim.' So you reply to the person "Don't I normally look nice and slim?" What was said as a compliment has become an insult through the distortion filter in your mind. If you have high self-worth and someone said that to you then you would take it as a compliment and thank him or her graciously and you would be happy and feel good. It may be you would distort something in another subject, depending on how you feel and what you believe about yourself.

Sometimes if someone says something in a certain tone of voice you may find yourself distorting the meaning because that tone to you says they are angry or irritated with you, when really they are not it is just their tone of voice. It is so easy to develop beliefs about yourself that are not good and this distortion filter helps with that process.

It depends upon your own self worth as to how you use the information that comes into your mind. If your self-worth is high then you will distort the information to suit your high self-worth and take the information in a positive light and use it well. If your self-worth is low then you will distort the information in a negative way and you will develop more and stronger negative beliefs about yourself and you will probably be quite defensive and easily upset.

**Your Conscious Mind
Values and Beliefs**

See

Hear   Touch

Taste

Filters

Smell

E
X
T
E
R
N
A
L

E
V
E
N
T
S

Thought

Delete

Distort

Generalise

Emotion

Physical

Behaviour

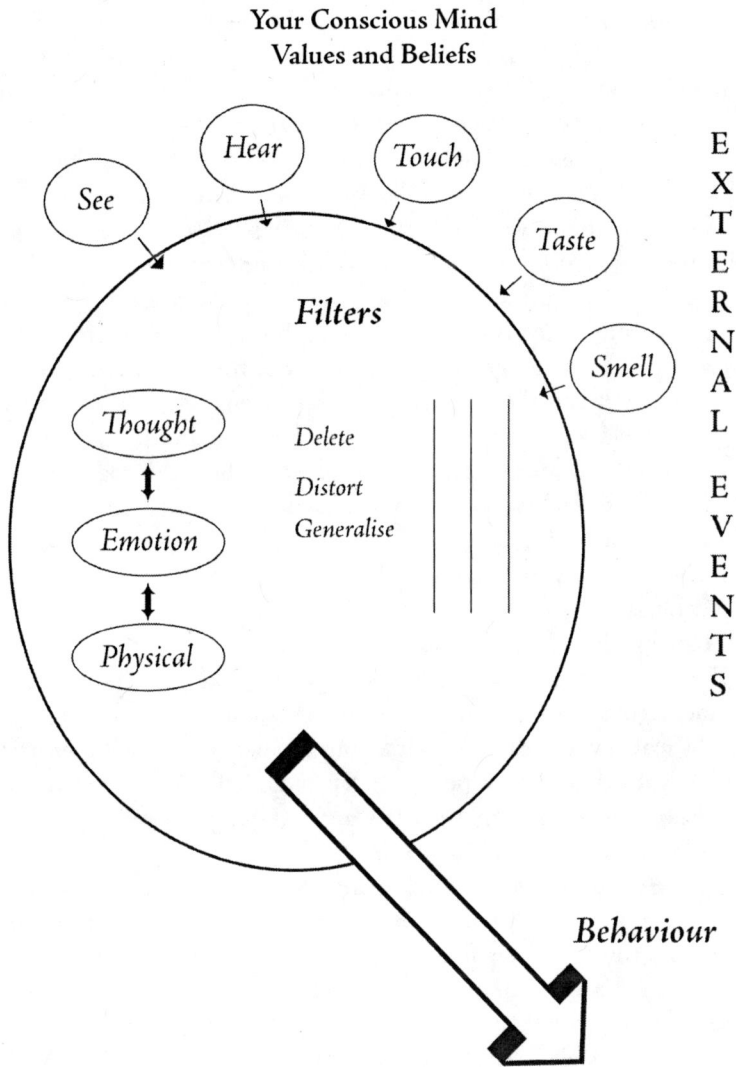

The next filter is to generalise; a lot of the information that comes in you will put into general categories, such as; if you see or hear the post-men come to the door that is a general thing that happens everyday and you will not do anything about it apart from pick up the post at sometime. The general category is the everyday things that happen that we file away and don't have to necessarily act upon all the time.

The most important of these filters and the one you need to watch is the distortion filter, this is the one that can cause the most damage to your self-belief and self-worth. Always use what you take in through your senses in a positive light and use it in a positive way, that way you will not be programming your mind in a negative way. The delete filter is also important in rejecting and deleting information that is negative or which you do not want to retain in your mind. Remember you can cultivate your mind just as you would a garden, you can decide what you will allow to grow in your mind and what you will delete.

Once this information has gone through the filters it then has an impact upon your thoughts (mind), your emotions (spirit) and your actions (body). This then has an impact upon your behaviour. Take the example above, someone has said 'You look nice and slim in the dress' you say to yourself 'don't I usually look nice and slim'. This can trigger a whole line of thoughts that are going on a downward spiral such as:

'I am fat and frumpy'
'I never have any nice clothes'
'My life stinks'
'I hate my life'

The behaviour that comes from this line of thinking will be negative, unmotivated and sullen, and it will be displayed in your body language and the words you speak. Of course you can change that by listening to what is really said and accepting it in a positive light and the behaviour and the body language will then display something very different, such as energy, smiles and positive words.

If you are not getting positive results in your life then you need to be aware of how you are receiving the information coming into your mind. Are you negatively filtering it and putting a negative twist onto it, and therefore programming your mind with negative thinking and behaviour?

Your mind is also divided into conscious and sub conscious, your thoughts being the conscious and your sub-conscious being your spirit. Your conscious mind is the mind that was just described in the above diagram; it takes in everything and filters it. It is your conscious mind that decides what will go through to your sub-conscious mind, and be stored there to be used as you need it. This is how the mind works, 'what you think about you bring about.' In his book 'The Millionaires Mindset' Gerry Roberts describes the conscious mind as the Captain of a ship giving orders to the crew, which is the sub-conscious mind.

Whatever you can consciously feel and hear going on in your head is being done by your conscious mind and your sub-conscious mind is taking orders from the conscious. The challenge is that the sub-conscious has no ability to reason or choose. If it gets an order it carries it out immediately, even the silent thoughts of the conscious mind become orders to the sub-conscious, this is why it is so important to know what you are thinking and why you are thinking it. This is why it is good to sit quietly each day for a few minutes so that you can learn to listen to what you are thinking and then change whatever is not building and improving you.

Your sub conscious is your power drive, it accepts everything your conscious mind accepts it has no power to accept or reject anything. Whatever your conscious mind takes in and accepts the sub-conscious mind accepts and then makes up a picture to fulfil it. If you have a picture of ill health in your mind, maybe you have been with someone who has a bad cold and you are thinking you may get a bad cold, then your sub-conscious mind will create that picture – you with a cold. Then sure enough your nose will start to run and your head will get heavy and before you know it you will have a bad cold just as you thought. It is the automatic part of you; it is the part that regulates your body, your breathing, temperature and other automatic responses that you need to activate all the time to stay alive. Your sub-conscious takes in everything you give it, it cannot tell the difference between realities and imagination. It is in your sub-conscious where your habits are, your automatic reactions to situations around you.

An example of this could be that someone has forgotten your birthday and you sit in the chair and think about why they forgot and before you know it your thoughts are, 'they don't like me' or 'why don't they like me anymore?' With each succeeding thought your emotions are going further and further down in a spiral until you are feeling really down and you also notice that your body is very heavy too.

Now this happened because you were thinking that they did not like you anymore and that thought sent a message to your sub-conscious that you had lost a friend and your sub-conscious sent a message to the emotions and the body and both responded in a downward turn.

Now if in your thoughts you had allowed yourself time to think that your friends might be busy or have some reason why they didn't get to you on your birthday. If instead of feeling sorry for yourself you thought about them and what could have kept them away on your birthday, you wouldn't have had time to feel sorry for yourself and your thoughts, emotions and body would not have gone through such a stressful situation.

There is another part of you besides your conscious and sub-conscious mind and that is your body. The physical side of you takes the physical actions and causes the physical results. Your body is actually much less important to how you feel and behave; it is in actual fact the very smallest part of who you are. This part of you expresses on the outside how you are on the inside, if you are feeling down and depressed it will show in your outward physical form. If you are feeling really positive and enthusiastic that will also show in your outward physical form.

Try this experiment with me now, think of something really sad, something that makes you feel down and upset, now as you are thinking these thoughts how does your body feel? What about your emotions how do they feel?

They will probably feel down and despondent, your body will feel heavy and lacking energy, this is showing how closely the thoughts, feelings and physical body are connected, you cannot affect one of them without the other two being affected.

Now think of something really exciting, something that has happened in the past that really makes you feel great even now after the event. How does that make you feel now? Your body becomes more energised and your emotions much happier. That is how easy it is to change your feelings and to lift yourself out of a situation that is draining you.

Change your thoughts and the way you see the situation.

There are many universal laws that can help you to create the life you desire and one of them is called the Law of Polarity, which means there is an opposite in everything. If something is sad there is also something happy about it, you just have to find it. Sometimes the apparent isn't so obvious at first and sometimes you have to work through the sadness until the happiness appears. Always looking for the good will help you to overcome adversity much quicker and to live a life that is happier and more satisfying.

An example of seeing the opposite quickly can be the story of the man who was sad because he had no shoes until he saw the man who had no feet. This put thing into perspective for him, now he was happy he had feet to wear shoes. You can be sad and upset about anything but it will not make you happy always wallowing in the sadness. To be grateful for what you already have is a good way of finding the opposite to the sad or bad part of experience.

Sometimes you may have to wait until you can see the good side of an experience. A good example of this is, when I left the keys in my car, left the car to go and unlock a building so that I could unload some goods. In the brief seconds it took to unlock the building, someone came and took my car. They just drove it away with all the goods in it. Now this was a bad situation, my car was gone and I didn't know if the insurance company would cover it because I had left the keys in it.

We got the car back a week later, with some damage but still drivable, the insurance company eventually decided they would cover the damage and it was taken away for repair. When the engineers looked at it they concluded that it would be more expensive to repair the car than it would be to replace it and the car was written off. We managed to buy a replacement car with only a third of the amount of miles on it than the car that was stolen. So even though the situation looked bad at first, a good thing came from it. There is a good and bad side to every situation and sometimes you have to wait awhile for the good to manifest itself. It is very easy to see the bad in any situation very quickly; it is always worth trying to see the good as well.

So if you go back to the window of your mind and check what state it is in when you have your children, you may find many beliefs etc blocking your view of the kind of world in which you wish to raise them. The only way to clean your window so as you can have a better view, is to change the way you perceive your life to be.

You may have a smear on your window that says, 'if your child is not progressing and doing as well as other children, then you are a bad mother.' This may cause you to constantly expect more from your child than your child is willing or able to give and this is will cause you to feel stress. If your child is at school they may not be progressing as well as you think they ought to be, maybe they are not learning to read and write as quickly as you thought they would. You are taking this information into your mind and distorting it in all kinds of ways that are causing you stress, such as, 'are they dyslexic?' 'do they have learning difficulties?' 'will they be the bottom of the class?' The problem with this is that your child will also pick up on your stress and thoughts. They will then distort this information they are absorbing, and start to feel some failure because they are not pleasing you.

To your window, you are adding more dirt and obscuring your view even more and also because the child is taking in information from you and distorting it to fit your belief, they also are adding dirt to their window and obscuring their view of the world. This is how beliefs are developed and how they can direct our lives and affect our destiny.

Life is very complex and there are many ways in which you can change your life by changing the way you think and feel and act. This can make you feel overwhelmed, the thought of changing anything that we habitually do can be terrifying but it does not have to be. You do not have to make massive changes overnight, it will be a matter first of all of noticing what it is that needs to be changed and you can do that by taking the time to analyse situations that are causing you some kind of stress or problem.

If you react to something in a way that makes you feel less than you are, for instance if someone says something about you or your child that immediately makes you feel defensive, and you react angrily, or you feel hurt and upset inside you can analyse these feelings and ask yourself how much truth there is in them.

Remember when someone else says something to you, unless it is an absolute truth and not changeable then it is only their opinion and that opinion has come from their mind that may have distorted the information they have taken in to fit their beliefs. So you are getting upset over something that someone else believes when it has gone through their filters and they have decided on what is right or wrong. Stop here and analyse the situation, do not let someone else's opinion direct your life, do not let someone else who does not know your situation as well as you do, affect how you feel and how you will act in your life. When you do this you are not living your life for yourself, you are caught up on the road of mass thinking. Because someone else thinks and feels one-way, you are caught in their road and walking their path.

If at this time you find yourself on the road of mass thinking there is a way to break free. It involves taking control of your own mind and thoughts, of using your own life and opportunities to push your way to the bright place you can see off to the left and to step out of mass thinking into your own thinking.

Chapter Eight

⌇

SIX MIND MUSCLES

Y ou have true genius within you, whoever you are, whatever you do, it is within you and you can bring it out of you by developing and using the six gifts you have been endowed with, to use the mind in a way which will manifest your true genius.

As a human being you have the most wonderful mind and that mind is made up of gifts that you have to help you to live your own life in your own way and to achieve whatever you set out to achieve. Your mind has been created with certain faculties that give it the ability to think and act independently of other peoples' minds; I call them muscles, because as with any muscle in the body when you exercise them they become stronger and more able to do their job better. Well it is the same with these faculties, the more you use them and develop them, the stronger they become and the more able you are of taking control of your thinking and therefore your life.

Let's look at the mass thinking we talked about at the end of the last chapter. Imagine if you will a road that stretches out into the distance and you can see no end to this road, it just keeps going, the further you get down the road the further it stretches out in front of you. On this road are crowds of people, all different people, some of them you recognise as friends and acquaintances, some you recognise from the TV, and many others you do not know. There are many people on the road and they jostle you, they carry you along and when you want to stop, you cannot, because of the mass of people who are walking down the road.

This can get very stressful because sometimes you see a road off to the right or left and you want to take that road, but try as you might you cannot get to the road because of the crowds around you. You try to push your way through the crowd but you get knocked down or pushed back by those surrounding you. The people in this crowd can be actual people in your life or they can be people you see on TV and other celebrity figures or they can be the beliefs you have that limit you to the road you are on.

Lets look first at all the people in your life who surround you and to an extent direct your life. You may have children or a spouse/partner, they are your responsibility in life and all your thinking, feeling and acting needs to work with and around them. If you see a road to the side that attracts your attention, it needs to be a road that will fit in and around your present responsibilities with regards to your family. It maybe that you can see and are attracted to a road signposted work and you have already decided that you will postpone going to work until your children are a little older. Just because you see it and are attracted to it does not mean you have to take it. I remember many years ago watching someone from my window, walking to get the bus to work, and the thought went through my mind as to how great it would be to go out of the house and mix with other adults and have some adult conversation. Then I went back to my children and realised my reasons for not working at this present time. 'The grass can sometimes look greener,' just keep focused on what you have already decided and desire.

Sometimes you may have made a decision to do one thing and then find that the road is not the right one for you, be flexible and make the change if it is best for you and your family. The important thing to remember is that you are travelling your road of life and as long as you are working within your boundaries, you decide which road you travel. If you are finding that you are stressed and feeling out of harmony in your life check out the road you are on, is it working for you and your family? It maybe that you are doing something that is out of harmony with your values. Many years ago my husband had a job that turned out to be out of alignment with what he believed and valued. He ended up giving that job up because the stress and disharmony were taking their toll on his health and his life.

The way you see something can cause you to feel stressed or out of harmony with your life. Before committing to any changes try looking at it from a different angle, remember there is usually more than one way to see something. It is the same with the masses of people you are travelling with down the road of life; some of the people around you will be family or friends. Make sure you are seeing the world through your eyes and not theirs, there will always be someone ready to give advice about what you should or shouldn't do or say. Remember they are seeing the situation through their window and not yours, they are seeing a different view of life from you so if you have to make any decisions make sure you are looking through your window when you make them.

It is your life and you are the only person who knows how you truly feel. Stop and analyse whether the road you are travelling on is right for you. If you are unhappy walking this road to nowhere with masses of people around you, then step out and get off this road and walk another way. Many times you can be guided and directed by what others are thinking and doing and it may not be right for you and your family, just because everyone else jumps off the cliff does not mean it is right for you to do so. Just because everyone else has the latest gadget or whatever is currently fashionable, it does not mean that you have to own it, do it or be it. Use the ability you have to direct your own life and to live within the boundaries you set for yourself whether those boundaries are larger or smaller than another's does not matter. They are your boundaries and you decide where they are and how far they extend and what they absorb.

So you find yourself on this road walking to nowhere in particular and you can see no end to the road, no actual destination. How can you step off the road and walk to the beat of your own drum, that is to walk your own road, thinking your own thoughts and making your own decisions about who and what and why you are doing what you are doing.

Think back to the earlier chapters where you learned about yourself and who you were, what you believed and how you could actually use your imagination to help you to visualise your future. To help you step off the road and live the life of your choosing, you have these mental muscles that you can develop. They will help you to think and act for yourself and to create the life you desire.

These muscles are perception, imagination, willpower, intuition, memory and reason. You can use each of these faculties or muscles to create your life, to detox your mind and to think independently and at last find a less stressful way to live, not just for you but for your family as well.

Perception

Your perception of life is the way you view your life to be and you can develop your ability to see your life in a different way, you can actually decide the circumstances you want. You can develop better ways to perceive your life and therefore to change your life if you want to.

Your perception is like the distortion filter in your mind, it is the way you are seeing and experiencing situations and events in your everyday life. Let's say when you were a child at school your teacher told you that you were no good at number work, maybe you had a difficult time grasping the concept of numbers or fractions of numbers. This problem may have come from someone else expressing his or her dislike of numbers because it was difficult. Therefore even before you learned numbers or fractions or algebra or whatever it is you find difficult, you had already perceived in your mind that it was going to be difficult and you would be no good at it.

It is your perception of numbers being difficult that holds you back, that stops you from being able to do it, not necessarily the fact that you cannot do it. I am not saying here that everyone who has difficulty with number has difficulty because of the way they view it, but for some of us it will be that way.

Let's take another example there is a young mother I know who seemes to have a charmed life, things just seem to happen for her. When I thought about this and watched her, I could see that because of her upbringing, which was in an affluent situation, she just expected everything to be there and she knew that what she wanted, she received. Her perception of life was that she would have an abundant life and everything she needed to live that life. She was walking her road according to her perception of life, which was that you could have everything you desire.

Can you see how the way you view things can make a difference in the way you live your life? If you have a circumstance you do not like or you are not enjoying, see if you can view it in a different way. Remember the woman I saw from my kitchen sink on her way to work, walking down the road toward the bus stop. At that time the thought

went through my mind how great it would be to get up and leave the
house and go to work. Then I decided to view it from another angle,
this woman had to get up early, get dressed up, made up, and go out
of the house on a cold morning, walk to a bus stop and travel to work
and then work for someone else all day, working to their agenda and
needs. I then looked at my own situation where I could take as long as
I liked to get ready, I could decide if I went out or stayed in, I had my
own agenda to work to and the flexibility to manage my own day. I was
happy to stand by the sink and let her go.

It is the way you view your life that gives you happiness and joy. If
you feel you could be happier then look at all the good things you already have in life and be thankful for them. Build on the good things,
focus your thoughts on what is right with your life and you will find
that they are the ones that get stronger and better. If you are focused on
what is wrong that is what you will build, your perception of life will
be miserable and you will find yourself more and more miserable. You
have a choice, you always have a choice in everything, use your choices
wisely and focus upon what is already good in your life, even if you
think your life is mostly bad, find the one good bit and focus upon it.

There is a saying that goes 'where your focus goes, your energy flows'
let your energy flow into building on the good parts of your life. As a
mother you will have ample opportunity to see happy, joy-filled mo-
ments with your children, build on these, let your children know how
happy they make you. All children will do something you don't like
or you don't want them to do for some reason, move them from that
behaviour to another behaviour in a way that does not make them feel
bad.

Remember that your children also have mental muscles and they
are building their perception of life each day through their own experiences; help them to focus on the good in their lives by praising them
and helping them to feel good about themselves.

Your perception of your life will have an affect upon your children's
perception of life. If you are angry they will perceive life to be angry,
if you are miserable they will perceive life to be miserable. You are the
example to your children; you can give them the greatest days of their
life by perceiving your life to be good and great.

Imagination

Your imagination can bring power flowing into your life or it can hold you in a dark room full of negativity. You have the ability to build a picture of your life and to make that picture as vivid and beautiful as you desire, on the other hand you also have the ability to make your life as dark and cold as you desire. The universal law of polarity says there is an equal opposite in all things, so if you perceive your life to be hard and miserable the universal law says it also has the capacity to be easy and happy. It all depends on the way you are looking at it.

How can your imagination make a difference to your life?

George Bernard Shaw said:

"You see things; and you say, 'Why?' But I dream things that never were; and say, 'Why not?'"

Your imagination is your ability to dream, to be able to see things that are not yet there and to say 'why not me?'

Many of you may have had your imagination muscle squashed as a child, being told to stop daydreaming and to get back to reality. If you watch a child at play they will use their own imagination and the experiences of their own short lives to make up games and playmates. Listen to your child when they are telling off one of their dolls and see how much they sound like yourself, they are lost in their world of play but they are using everyday language and tonality that they have heard around them.

You can use your imagination to attract to you what you desire. When in your imagination you see yourself as a calm and gentle mother you are more likely to be calm and gentle than anything else. Let your imagination be your friend and let it work for you, use it to create the life you desire, when you can actually see what you want it is so much easier to go out and get it.

When your children are using their imagination and dreaming of flying through space in a space ship let them keep dreaming, let their imagination grow and develop so that they can one day fulfil their own purpose in life. When I was a child if you had a dream or a big idea you were laughed at. I had a cousin who would go to great lengths to find out how much it would cost to buy a helicopter or a ship. He was laughed to scorn and many people told him he was crazy, how wrong they were. There was no harm in him enquiring after such things, the harm was in other peoples inability to use their own imagination if only to dream of such things.

There are many, many people whom the world should be thankful for today who let their imaginations work to develop many of the great inventions we now have. Can you imagine someone thinking up the computer? I am sure when computers were the size of a room someone must have sat there looking at this massive computer and thinking wouldn't it be good if you could have a computer on your desk.

As a mother you can use your imagination in many ways, you can see your children as successful adults making their own way in the world, you can see your home just as you would like it to be and then use that picture to make it that way. Make sure whatever you are imagining that it serves yourself and others and causes no harm to anyone else.

When you know what you want, when you have a picture of it in your imagination you can then go about taking the steps to get it. It is so much easier to go for something you can see even if it is only in the minds eye, have this vivid picture and then step by step start taking the steps it will take to receive whatever it is into your life.

Make your imagination your friend and let it inspire and lift you to heights of thinking and working that give you the freedom to live with joy and happiness. Joy and happiness do not come with money they come with the effort you make to live a life that is in line with the values you have. Your imagination will help you to get what you want in life, as you visualise it in your mind you will be able to see yourself already in possession of it and this will give motivation and determination to develop the picture into reality.

Willpower

This is the muscle that allows you to focus and concentrate on whatever you are imagining. You can bring it to reality! Many of you will say I have no willpower when it comes to achieving a certain goal, we all have willpower it just needs developing and making stronger in your life. You may find you have strong willpower in one thing and then weak willpower in something else. You will need to strengthen your willpower in what ever it is you are trying to achieve, as you do you will find you have the ability to achieve it.

As a mother you will have the opportunity everyday to strengthen your will. Think of a time when you might start to feel irritable about something, it maybe that your child has done something you have asked them not to do. Now you have a choice, you can get annoyed and even lose your temper with them and shout and rant at them, or you can use your willpower to control your irritability and speak to them in tones that are firm but loving. Therefore you are giving your child the example that even though people do not always do what you want them to do there are good ways of dealing with it.

Exercising and developing your willpower will give you control over your life; it will help you to feel stronger and more able. It is not a great show of ability on the outside but a quiet resolve on the inside of you to be the best you can be, to give out to others a solid, controlled picture of you and who you are. People from all walks of life will gravitate to someone who is in control of their own thoughts, words and actions; they will want to be around you and will learn from you because you have the presence of someone who knows who they are and what they are about.

Your willpower can make you strong in your everyday life, not just in some things but in everything, as you learn to control your emotions and appetites and display positive behaviour you will also show wisdom and maturity and you will attract people who desire the same behaviour.

Having a strong body is good because it enables you to do many more things than you could do if you were weak. Having a strong mind is the same; it enables you to face great challenges in life and to work through them whilst maintaining some balance in your life.

How will a strong willpower help you as a mother? It will give you the ability to be strong when your child is pestering you for something. Many times mothers give in for the sake of peace and quiet. If you have developed your willpower you will be able to adhere to your own rules. You will be able to refocus your child's want on to something they can have and thereby satisfying the child and yourself by not giving in and weakening your resolve.

There is a great need for a mother to help her child to gain discipline in their life and discipline is really another word for willpower. Discipline is not about punishment; it is about learning and developing an ability to follow a setline of behaviour or thinking. When a child develops discipline or willpower they will know there are boundaries within which they can act.

Children have got great willpower within them and I learned very early it is not good to go head to head with a child on the willpower stakes; they will win unless you use force to break their will. As a mother you do not want to break your child's will. You want to help them to develop it in a disciplined way, to know that there are boundaries as to how far they can go with certain behaviour. As you teach your child this they will accept it quite freely and even be grateful for it. It will give them stability in their life and help them to live and play with confidence because they know what they can do and what they can't do.

It is better for the child to learn this at home, to learn to accept and work within the rules of the home, than when they go to school. They will be more prepared to accept and work within the rules of the school. The willpower you develop as a mother at home with children will serve you well for the rest of your life; it will help you when you are ready to go back out into the world of work, knowing that you have the strength of character and discipline to adapt to a new environment and opportunities, to learn and develop new skills which will require all the willpower you have.

Intuition

Your intuition is that feeling in your gut that something is either happening now or is about to happen. It is the way you can tell if someone is telling the truth or if someone is not quite telling you all they need to. As a mother developing this 'muscle' will be of great benefit to you. Your children may not always tell you everything that is happening to them and it is your intuition that can pick up on this and save you and your child from suffering more than you have to.

Intuition is not something you can see or touch; it is a feeling or an insight that something is good or bad, right or wrong. Sometimes people can have something that is bothering them but they cannot express it and therefore stay quiet and keep the problem to themselves. You can use your intuition to recognise this, especially in your children; the closer you are to someone in this situation the better you will be able to see from their behaviour that there may be something bothering them.

Pay close attention to your children from when they are born; learn to know them, their reactions and habits. If you see a change in these then you might feel there is something bothering them that they need to speak about. Much heartbreak can be saved when an intuitive person gently leads another to talk about what is disturbing them. As you develop your intuition your child again will follow your example and develop and use their intuition as they grow up to help others.

Memory

Your memory is the place within your mind where you store everything you have taken in through your five sense and have not deleted. That is a lot of information and you do not forget any of it, you have a perfect memory, it is the recall of the information that does not always work, as you would like it to.

To develop this tool you need to use it, many of us want to be better at remembering names and events that will help us later on when we need to recall the name of someone you met a while ago. A mother especially will need to develop her memory to recall where items are in the home. It can be time consuming and annoying to have to keep looking in lots of places to find things you have put away. One way to do this is to be organised and have a place for everything, that way you do not have to remember the same thing in many different ways. You just have to remember where you keep that particular item you are looking for. A hairbrush for instance. "A place for everything and everything in its place."

A way of training your memory and building its capacity is to use association, if you meet someone for the first time and want to remember their name, associate it with something else, if you meet someone whose name is Jill you may associate the name with Jack and Jill in the nursery rhyme, next time you need the name her face will say 'Jack and Jill' to you.

You can develop your memory by using it, as with any muscle, do exercises and games that require you to use your memory. Remembering numbers in twos and threes can be helpful. Telephone numbers with seven or eight digits can be difficult to remember but in groups of two or three it is easier. When your children are at school they will be learning lots of things and you can use your memory to remember some of the things they are learning like the times tables or English comprehension.

As a mother your memory will be called upon to remember many things that will help you in all the other areas of your life, when you can remember things it will help your confidence when with other people. You will be constantly called upon to remember facts and figures. If your child is ill you will have to remember many things about the child and the symptoms when you visit the doctor. If when you decide to go to work or start a business you will need a great memory to remember all the facts and figures that will be needed constantly.

Use the time you have everyday to develop this muscle, as you are out walking you can take note of things along the route and when you return you can try and remember as many things as possible that you saw on the walk. You can fit this into your everyday life, as you walk to school or the shops. If you don't walk a lot you can remember the order of how the vegetables were laid out in the greengrocers. There are lots of things you can do to develop your memory, a favourite one for me is to memorise some thing everyday, a small quote or verse of something, developing the habit of using your memory will pay off later in life.

Reason

Your reasoning power is very important to you in your everyday life, it is your power to accept or reject information that comes into your mind. You use your reasoning to decide whether you need the information, whether you agree with the information and whether the information is good for you or bad for you.

Think about the window of your life that you are looking out of everyday, your reasoning power can be what you use to clean that window. Not everything that is thrown at that window has to stay on it; you can use your reasoning muscle to clean some of it off. Let's say someone says something to you that does not lift and inspire you, in fact it makes you feel really bad. You now have a choice to let it stay on your window or obliterate it, you can think about it and let it play on your mind and continue to make you feel bad, or you can clean it off your window, let it go and reject it completely as an untruth.

You do not have to accept everything that other people think and say, you have the ability to reason with and decide if it is what you believe and if it is not you can let it go and not think about it. Remember unless it is an absolute truth, like knowing the sun will rise in the east tomorrow, then whatever someone else says to you it is only their opinion of what they think and feel. Therefore you do not have to accept it; you can reject and delete it. So many people today are carrying burdens put there by other peoples' opinions. If you do not like it, if it does not fit you then don't accept it, clean it from the window of your mind. Of course if you do feel there is something you could learn from it then learn it and let it go, do not allow someone else's opinion to direct your life, develop your own beliefs and values to create the life you desire.

I had a friend who listened to her cousin; she believed everything her cousin said and lived by it. This cousin was happily married with children, which was what my friend wanted too. Every time my friend got a boyfriend, she would talk to her cousin and tell her how great she felt, then her cousin would start to tell her to be careful, setting seeds of mistrust into her mind, eventually my friend would lose these boyfriends because she couldn't trust them and this showed in her relationship with them.

My friend was letting someone else direct her life by accepting her cousin's opinion of her boyfriends instead of using her own reasoning power. This is your life, you have the tools and opportunities to live it well, do not take in everything you see and hear in one day and accept it as truth, be discerning and weed out all that you don't agree with and let it go. You can start to clean your own window by letting go of the many beliefs that do not fit you and who you are.

You live in a world that is dominated by the media; remember when you read an article in a newspaper or magazine it is not an absolute truth but it is the opinion of the person who wrote it. The facts may be there but they will be coloured by the values and beliefs of the person who wrote it. Just as this book is coloured by my beliefs that mothers are the greatest people on earth and should be valued as such. You do not have to take my opinion of that but you can reason it out for yourself and make your own decision as to what you will believe and not believe.

As your children grow older and start to develop their own mental muscles they will develop their own opinions and beliefs, sometimes they will not be the same as yours and this is where you will need to use all your mental muscles to develop a relationship with which you can both enjoy life respecting each other's choices.

Your mind is your most precious commodity, it is where you will plant the seeds that will grow into plants to adorn your life and make it a beautiful and fruitful place.

James Allen in his book 'As A Man Thinketh' said

"A man's mind may be likened to a garden, which may be intelligently cultivated or allowed to run wild; but whether cultivated or neglected, it must, and will bring forth. If no useful seeds are put into it, then an abundance of useless weed-seeds will fall therein, and will continue to produce their kind."

Cultivate your mind by filling it with knowledge and information that will allow it to grow and give you all the confidence, strength and ability you need to live the life you aspire to. It is your choice, there is always a choice, if you want to live your life through someone else, letting others direct you thinking, then you can get that from TV, magazines and other media or you can think for yourself and develop your own mental muscles to create the life you want for yourself.

You do not and will not change everything over night; it will be a process of taking one small step after another until you start to see change occurring in your life. Look at your window. What beliefs are blocking the view of your life? Start by changing them and developing new beliefs that lift and inspire you. If you are not sure what you want in life then take the time to be still and to listen to yourself, listen to how you feel about different things in life. When you are in a group, sit back and listen to the conversation, how do you feel about it? Does it uplift you? Does it make you feel good? Develop your own values, and the things you stand for. Gain strength each day by travelling in the direction you believe is right for you.

Your children will grow and find stability in your stability, they need you to help them find direction, if you are meandering all over the place and have no firm direction your children will also be like this and that is when they might get pulled into a direction that may not be good for them. Be strong in your life and you will pass that strength to your children.

Chapter Nine

❧

SEVEN STEPS TO SELF-MASTERY

THE beautiful planet you live on is very complex and holds a life form that is very complex, it is the human race. That is you and I, and everyone else, you may think that life can be difficult in different ways; some may find it physically hard whilst others find it emotionally hard. Then there are others who on the surface seem to sail through life with a good wind behind them and always get to where they plan to go.

So what makes the difference between all people, what is it that gives some people a seemingly easy life and others a life of hardship?

There are many aspects of life to consider in this question and one of them could be hereditary. What have you inherited from your parents, grandparents and even further back, not just in looks and temperament but also in circumstances and environment? There is bound to be something that affects your life that has come in one of these ways and this is linked to the way your life is influenced and that is what I call the 'traditions of the fathers'.

Going back in time over the centuries there has been a division of classes; I am reminded of a TV program we called 'Upstairs Downstairs'. It was about the lives of two separate classes of people, those who lived upstairs, who gave the orders and demands, and those who lived downstairs who fulfilled the orders and demands. This division of classes led to a way of thinking that kept the two classes of people at a distance. The people downstairs felt that they were not supposed to think, just carry out orders, and be subservient to those upstairs. The people upstairs felt that they were the successful ones and to stay successful they had to keep the people downstairs in their place as servants, and not allow them to think and feel for themselves.

Fortunately in today's enlightened society things have moved on and although there is still a division between employee and employer. It is hoped that today's employers are much more enlightened and that they treat their employees as equals, as people who are unique in their experience and view of life and should therefore be allowed to contribute to all life. Everyone in the world has the right of freedom to think and feel, as they believe. If life and freedom are to be maintained and people are to live happy and fulfilled lives it is important that individuals can express themselves in ways that make them feel good about themselves and their opportunity to live the lives they desire.

How far have we come in today's society from those days of 'Upstairs Downstairs'? In the physical sense there has been progress, even if people have servants nowadays there is a tendency to treat those people with dignity. They are paid decent salaries and have work policies and procedures that protect them from being exploited.

What about the rest of the people?

In today's world of work there are laws and policies that protect from exploitation and it seems that in the physical sense there is equality. That is until you come to examine the thinking of people and this is where the traditions of the fathers come in. As time has moved on and working conditions improved people do not necessarily change their thinking at the same rate. Many people and in particular the people born in the baby boom era, between 1946 and 1964 may still be working with beliefs that they are not worthy of success and that they are still in the servant quarters. This is because of beliefs and ideas that have been handed down through generations and although they are not as strong and they are not enforced, they still serve to repress people and stop them from reaching their potential.

Examine your own thoughts and feelings about who you are and what you can achieve. If the opportunity arose enabling you to be very successful and to have all that success brings, meaning money, fame and attention, how would you handle it? Think of some of the stars and celebrities of the past and present, how they handle success? Some do handle it well, but many you hear and read about are not handling the pressure of being famous, rich, or successful and you may wonder why not. I am sure with each person the reason is different and some of it could be the result of their own thoughts and feelings of inadequacy also being out of their 'depth,' having risen above the 'station' they had been given to believe by the 'traditions of the fathers' was theirs.

Everyone today has the right and opportunity to be successful; it is accepting that right and aligning your thoughts with the principles of success and how to achieve it. Many people will not achieve success in life because their thinking is still in that class division and to be successful you have to change your way of thinking. We have already talked about how the mind works and how you can change your thoughts to achieve all things.

In this chapter you are reading about at the various steps that lead to self-mastery and success and where you are on the ladder to successful thinking and living. As we discuss the various levels take the time to think about you and where you are now on this ladder, this will help you to know who you are and when you know that, you can start to climb the ladder one step at a time.

Level One Victim

This is the fight or flight level, you are very much pushed around by life, you react to situations and feel you have no control over what happens to you. You will feel trapped by circumstance and will feel you have no choice in life. This is the life you were born to, your station in life and there is nothing you can do to change it. Your level of thinking is very closed and your mind cannot conceive of anything other than what and who you are now and what life has to offer.

If people try to help or make a suggestion you will have an excuse as to why you cannot do this or that. You will feel and act like a victim, it will always be someone else's fault as to why you are in your present circumstances. This is a level of not accepting responsibility for your actions and circumstances; it is a level where you are blinded by the 'traditions of your fathers'. The beliefs given to you and to your parents and their parents in turn still have a hold on you and if success came to you now at this level you would do something to sabotage it because your thinking and your mind would not be able to handle it.

To rise above this level you will need to start to take responsibility for your actions and to lift your thinking to a level of 'I can' instead of 'I can't'. If you want to change, if you want to have better circumstances then that change has to come from you, no one else can change for you. It is your life and your responsibility and you can make that change. Start now by accepting one thing that you can do today that will make a difference to your life, it does not have to be a big thing it can be as small as saying 'I can change', 'I can improve my circumstances'. Repeating this over and over again will have an affect on your outlook on life.

Another thing you can try is, the very next time a situation occurs when you would normally get angry or upset, stop and take the time to choose an action. If your child does something that is wrong and you can feel anger rising up inside you, stop for a minute, even a few seconds and choose a different response. Choose to talk and explain why you do not want them to do what they are doing and explain your reasons. This will help you to rise above the reactionary stage and you will find it easier in time to always act this way. Remember between situation and action or reaction there is a space for choice, you just have to stop long enough to allow yourself to choose an action.

Humans are creatures of habit and it is your habits that make up your life, it is the habit of reacting that causes you to do the things you do. To get past this you need to form new habits, ones that will serve you better and make life much more pleasant and happier. A habit is simply an action or a thought that you do repeatedly, so if you want to stop reacting angrily to situations you must develop the habit of stopping and choosing your actions. That sounds very easy to write or speak about and I know it is not easy to do, but like any habit, it gets easier the more you repeat it.

Use the information in the previous chapter on willpower and imagination; you can use the willpower to develop the focus and concentration you need to stick with the new habit, and the imagination you can use to see a new you in your minds eye. See the person you want to become and then keep that picture there, make it as vivid as you can and strengthen it by visualising it several times each day.

Use the information in the previous chapters to help you to rise above this level to the next level of the masses.

Level Two Masses

As the name of this level suggests this is where most people are living, with the masses in one way of mass thinking, it is being conditioned to

conform to the 'follow the crowd' mentality. People are not really thinking for themselves but are doing whatever they do because it is what is
expected or what everyone else is doing.

There are several ways in which people tend to follow the masses
and one of them is fashion, some fashion guru somewhere decides that
they would like a certain colour and style to be in this year and they put
it in the magazines and on the cat walks and the people accept it. The
factories make it, the shops sell it, and people wear it and all because
someone decided that was going to be the style; this is most frustrating
when you decide that you want something that is not the 'in' colour.

What about the media? They keep the people thinking and feeling
just like they are, they write negatively about something, the people
read it and they in turn feel the negativity and think that everything
is like that. Remember there is the law of polarity that says there is an
equal opposite in all things so if something has the power to be negative it also has the power to be positive. People living on the level of the
masses are influenced by what they see on TV, hear on radio, what they
read in newspapers and magazines and any other form of communication out there.

You live in a world full of possibility, opportunity is there for anyone who wants to take advantage of it, living on this level will close
your mind to possibility and opportunity, you can change that, you can
lift yourself and your thinking to a greater level. As a mother you will
benefit your child or children when they see you living above the level
of the masses, they will benefit from seeing your example of living and
from the circumstances you create from your higher thinking.

Let me tell you of my vision for a better world for everyone.

For some years now I have had this vision of walking down a road,
hemmed in on every side by other people, not able to move one way or
the other but only being pressed by the crowd to travel this road. Every
so often I would catch a glimpse of a brighter place just to the left of
me, I would try to move toward the brighter place but every time I was
pushed back unable to move in the direction I wanted to go. I kept getting the glimpses of something better and I continued to push toward
them, eventually I gained enough strength, courage, self awareness and
confidence that I finally was able to break free from the masses and
discover a whole new and exciting life.

I discovered talents I did not know I had; I discovered opportunities that were waiting for me. Most of all I discovered my wonderful self, my mind and potential that had lain untapped and dormant for so long, previous successes that I had not recognised - my own needs that were waiting to be filled.

My vision now is to help you to discover for yourself what I discovered about myself and to help you to open your mind to the possibility that there is more out there for you than you presently have in your life and to start to develop your potential, to become more self aware and happier.

If you feel you are on this level now then commit yourself to change, use the information in this book to change the way you think, feel, and act. In that way you will be able to make the small everyday changes that build up into massive change in thought, emotion and physical circumstances.

Ask yourself what beliefs you have that limit you, that do not serve you at all and take one belief at a time and work with it until you have changed it. In the first part of this book you read about strategies and tools you can use to change the way you see yourself and beliefs you have about yourself, use them and also develop your mental muscles to allow change to take place.

You are unique, there is no one else in the world like you, your thoughts your beliefs and experiences are yours and no one else will ever have the exact same experience as you do. Celebrate your uniqueness, enjoy it and be happy with it, do not compare yourself to anyone because you may find you are better at something than one person but there will always be someone better at something else than you. You are incomparable, you do not need to be the same as someone else, you are an individual with individual likes and dislikes, your tastes are different to others, so celebrate your difference do not hide it, use it to lift and inspire you to move onwards and upwards and your children will thank you for it.

Let me tell you of an experience I had with one of my sons. One day he came home from school and asked me why we (his father and I) had to be so different. We were different in the fact that we had a deep religious belief and as part of that belief we did not drink alcohol and would not frequent public houses. He said he respected that we did not drink but can we go to the 'pub' and just sit and chat with the other mums and dads who were there. I asked him if he could really see us, his mum and dad, it that kind of a surrounding? I appreciated that he wanted to be the same as his friends and to be with his friends as they were playing around the pub-yard why their parents were drinking and socialising but he realised that it was not in line with who we were or our beliefs and values. I pointed out to him that the pressure he was feeling from his peers to conform was not necessarily good and that he could still have his friends without having to conform to everything they said or did. He happily accepted that in our way we were different and would not conform to the masses. Now he is older he appreciates that difference and has embraced it himself.

As a mother you have children who are dealing with everyday pressures from their peers, if they are a little different in some way that is good for them, help them to celebrate that difference and to build upon it. Do not be afraid to be different yourself and let your children see your difference; it will help them to think on a higher level than the masses.

Level Three Aspiration

This is a level of feeling, you have no clear picture of who you are but you have a feeling of their being something more to you than what you are presently experiencing. A desire deep inside of you that wants to come out but is not sure how or even what it is. This gives you a glimpse of my vision as I was walking down the road of the masses.

To develop this level take time to sit quietly and listen, listen to yourself and to what you are thinking. Your mind will probably jump around quite a lot when you first start trying to do this, keep going and keep working at it until you start to feel and to know what you are thinking and feeling. Focus your mind on your breathing, as you take deep breathes from your abdomen watch your abdomen as it rises and falls with each inhalation and exhalation. As you focus your thoughts upon you and who you are, what you feel and what you want, you will eventually be able to hear yourself and become aware of your desires.

At this level you are moving out of the masses and you will have a lot to leave behind, moving from one level to the next is not an overnight experience, it takes time and effort to change the way you think. Remember you are walking down a road hemmed in on every side by people, some of these people will be people quite close to you in every-

day life and they will not want you to change because if you change it
will change life for them and it may also threaten them with change.

At this level you may well meet opposition, expect it, watch for it
and be prepared for it, keep moving to the side of the road and every
time you are pushed back into the masses get up and try again, it will
get a little easier with each try. Don't give up and think 'poor me' and
feel sorry for yourself, there is a danger here you may fall back into
victim mode and blame circumstance and people for not being able
to change and grow. Don't do it, keep that vision of a better life and a
better world for you and your family, keep as far as you can from the
naysayers, those people who tell you it cannot be done, that you should
be happy with what you have. If they are family and you cannot avoid
them, then strengthen your resolve when you are around them to be
strong, and you will quietly go forward and practise getting to know
yourself and your aspirations.

Level Four Individual

You are gaining knowledge about yourself that is allowing you to think
and feel as an individual and you have a desire to express your uniqueness in your thoughts and actions. You are developing an awareness of
you and your world and that there never has been anyone who thinks
and feels and acts the way you do. This awareness opens your mind to
other possibilities that you may have abilities that you have not realised
and that this time can be the beginning of a journey into the realms of
thoughts and possibility.

You are half way up a mountain of discovery and you may catch
glimpses now of the peak of that mountain. You are feeling that belief
in yourself that you can achieve, you can be that person that lies deep
inside of you. Keep your focus, know that the peak is there and attainable, you can keep moving at the level you are to attain it. Be patient
and know that each level needs to be worked through so you can enjoy
and manage the next level, it is your birthright to develop your character and potential to be the best you can.

Your desires and insights into your own self are becoming clearer
and you are anxious to achieve them, to do this you are now taking
risks in being you, the person you know you are. You have stepped off
the road, a great accomplishment, to push past the crowds that would

hold you down with them, trudging the road of mass living. Celebrate your accomplishment, pat yourself on the back, you can now explore the brighter place you could see from the road and you can enjoy the fruits of the actions you took to get here.

As you enjoy being on this level of awareness acknowledge others still striving to get here, or those who have no idea of the existence of another level of thinking and living. They, like you, still need others to lift and inspire them that they might one day leave the realm of the masses and follow you. It is important that in your achievement you remember that responsibility also comes, the responsibility to act in a way that will give others the desire to move forwards and upwards.

Take care that you stay focused and move forward even in small degrees; you have not made it yet there is still work to be done. Complacency here would be dangerous, it could be the means of you going backwards towards the road of the masses, remember there will still be people on the road who miss your company and will be trying to get you to come back and be the person they enjoyed being around. Do not fall into their thinking; instead do what you can to bring them to you, to lift their thinking and actions to a higher existence.

Be strong in your thoughts, getting to know who you are is giving you the strength you need to keep going, to keep on discovering hidden levels within yourself, this discovery is exciting and empowering, continue to study and read empowering books and listen to empowering material. Do not get caught up with the existence of the masses, live your own life and forget what is happening in your favourite soap, I hope by now you have left that behind and are creating your own life above the level of soap.

You are unique, you are special as is everyone else and when they realise it they will wonder how they ever found any satisfaction in living on the level of the masses.

Level Five Discipline

This is a level of consolidation, a level where you focus your attention on making sure you are reprogramming your mind to bring the results your desire in your life.

Discipline is not about punishment, it is not about conditioning yourself to be or do something. Discipline is about drawing yourself a line and then following that line to accomplishment.

If you think of the word discipline and break it down into two words it makes disciple and line, a disciple is a follower, Jesus Christ has disciples, Buddha, Mahatma Ghandi have disciples, people who follow them and their teachings, so a disciple is a follower and the last word is line, the word discipline means to follow the line.

Draw yourself a line from where you are now to where you want to be and then follow that line closely, if you veer from it get back on it, the line will still be there as long as you are following it.

Imagine you have a desire that you have nurtured and developed and you are ready to achieve it, acknowledge where you are at the beginning of the line and where or what you want to be at the end of the line. That is to know what you want and to have a specific goal in mind, now you can draw a straight line to whatever you want to do, be, or have in your life.

Break down your desire into sections so you can make marks along the line to measure your success as you go along, this will be important to keep you motivated toward your success. Make sure that what you want to do, be, or have, is attainable for you, taking into account any circumstances you have. To be a fighter jet pilot may not be attainable for you if you have toddlers that need you at home, so when you are drawing your line ensure that you take into account your circumstances.

Remember as you are moving toward self-mastery you are doing it along with everything within your life. If you have responsibilities to another person or people you cannot dissolve those responsibilities, they are a part of you and your life and need to be taken with you to whatever level you aspire to. As you improve and develop your own life you will be improving and developing the lives of those around you, particularly children.

As a mother you have the ability to guide and direct your children's lives and whatever knowledge and intelligence you attain to in this life will serve them in their lives. As you develop your ability to discipline yourself you will find ways to help your children to be more disciplined, you will naturally pass your experience and knowledge to your children through your teaching and most of all through your example.

You have the greatest opportunity in the world to teach and make a difference to others; within your own home you can be disciplined in your approach to life and to situations that will allow growth for all members of the household. Become the person you feel is inside of you, as you have advanced thorough the levels of new growth you have learned many things about yourself, as you advance through this level and learn to follow through on your desires you will be gaining strength and character that will keep you focused on achieving your greatest desires.

Level Six Experience

Over the last five levels or from wherever you started on this journey, if it wasn't at level one, you have learned many new things about yourself and about the world you live in, you will have felt the power of living in a way that is focused on achievement and progress and also of understanding and compassion.

You will have experienced many emotions as you have progressed toward who you are today, you may have many times wanted to give up and crawl backward to where you came from, where the world was safe and you didn't have to risk anything, where it was comfortable and you could curl up and sleep. You have attained new knowledge along the way about yourself and how your mind works, about the world and how it works and with any knowledge comes new life.

Every time you learn something new, your life changes, you are not the same person because you know something more than you did before, it is your choice to act upon this new knowledge, it is there and it has changed you if only a little. On the level of experience you are ready to take all the information you have gathered about yourself and life and step out with it into action

It is your right to be the best you can be and if you can feel there is something better for you and you have a desire for it, then it is your right to go forward and achieve it, to make the effort it takes to come and take it, whatever it is. As you keep trying to go forward remember that there are laws in the universe that will help you, the law of cause and effect says that if you take a certain action there will be an effect. If you put your hand into the fire (cause) you will get burned (effect). So with every positive action you take to rise to your aspiration (cause) you will receive a positive result (effect), the bigger the action the bigger the result.

As you keep working at this level your confidence will grow and the following chart shows you the confidence cycle; this is how you achieve what you want. With each successful cycle your confidence grows and you, step by step achieve your goal and change your life. You have your vision and from that you set yourself a goal. Something you want to achieve, now you know what you want you have the confidence to take steps toward it. It is very important that you have a vision of something to aim for, remember you are on a journey and knowing where you are going will make it so much easier to reach your destination. Knowing what you want is to know where you are going.

This is the stage where the desire you felt at the beginning of your journey will bear fruit, you will put it into action and gain results, from those results you will gain feedback and from that feedback you will respond with more action or with new knowledge, you will change your desire or action.

Use this cycle to achieve whatever you desire, if you want to be slim fit and healthy then use this cycle to do it. Make yourself a plan; you may want to lose two stone in weight and become much fitter and healthier, to do this you are going to watch what you are eating and you are going to take regular exercise. To set yourself this goal or outcome you can write it down in a specific way so as you can read it daily and stay focused upon your desire.

Confidence Cycle

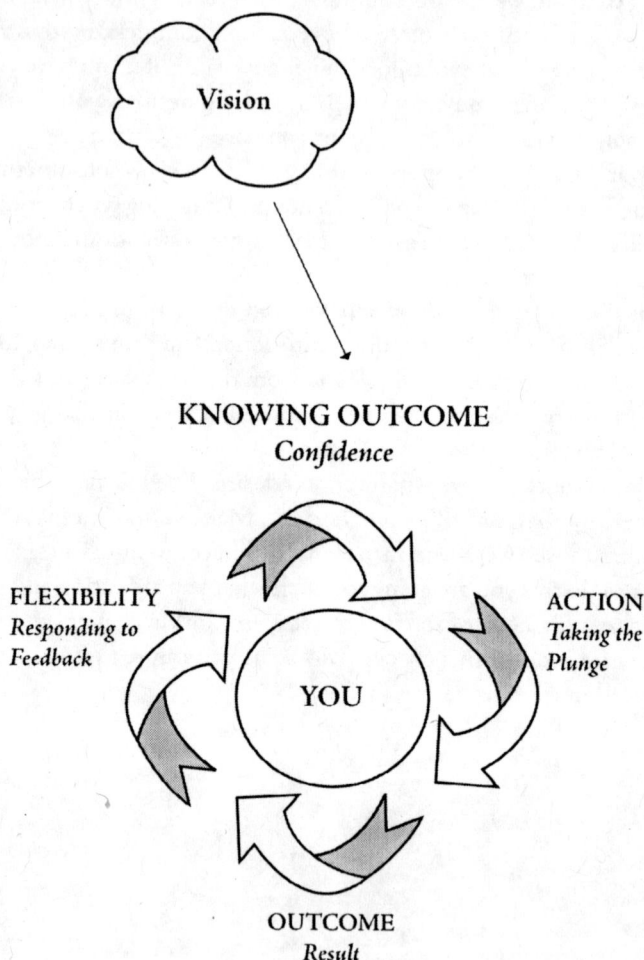

Vision

KNOWING OUTCOME
Confidence

FLEXIBILITY
*Responding to
Feedback*

YOU

ACTION
*Taking the
Plunge*

OUTCOME
Result

Goal:
I am slim, fit and healthy and I have achieved losing two stones in
weight in six months and so through exercise I can now swim 1 mile,
64 lengths in 45 minutes.
   This is a **SMART** goal

Specific - You are saying exactly what you want to achieve.

Measurable - In six months you can lose one pound of weight each week for 26 weeks. At the beginning you may lose more to make up the other 2 pounds.

Attainable - One pound a week is quite possible for someone watching their food intake. Also exercise to fit your present health levels.

Realistic - It is something you can do around your circumstances, if you cannot go swimming you could walk briskly for two miles each day particularly if you have a toddler or baby to push around. This will work well, and you could do toning exercises in the home.

Timeframe – you have given yourself six months to achieve your desired.

As you set goals and achieve them your level of experience is growing and your confidence is high, you feel great about yourself and you know you can achieve whatever you put your mind to. You have discovered hidden reservoirs of strength, tenacity and determination that will take you toward anything you desire to achieve in your life.

You see and feel success and a great happiness that comes from taking control of your life and your own mind and as you continue to achieve you step up to self- mastery.

Level Seven Self Mastery

Self-Mastery is not about having, being and doing everything, it is about being in control of your thoughts your emotions and your life. You do not have to be rich or have any great educational achievements, you do not have to be in a high office or have achieved some great thing. Self-Mastery is about you and who you know you are and what you are about.

Self-worth could be another name for self-mastery, it is the pinnacle of life to know who you are and what you stand for in any situation, where even if you lose everything you have achieved you can stand tall and know that you are still a person of great worth and what you stand for is still there and intact.

It is the character you have forged on your journey to this place which counts, not the many achievements or success, money or things you have accumulated, it is your ability to empathise with others and to lift and inspire others to reach out and take that journey of self-mastery themselves and to feel their achievement in gaining self- mastery.

As a mother you can do this for your child, in school they will be taught what to think, they will be taught great knowledge that will help them in life. You as their mother will have the opportunity to teach them greater things; you can teach them how to think. How to use their mental muscles to develop the character and self-worth that will help them to make a difference to their world. No two people view the world in the same way, so everyone has an equal chance of impressing themselves and their character upon the world for good or for evil.

Whoever you are, whatever your circumstances you can rise above the turmoil of this world to greater heights of accomplishment and joy. It is your right as a human being to live to the highest possible level of existence; you are the only person who can make that journey for you. Embrace the challenge, take the plunge and enjoy the delights of progress and achievement, you can do anything you put your mind to, decide at what level you are at now and move onward and upward toward total mastery of yourself and become the person that is hidden deep beneath the many layers of previous experience.

It matters not what you have experienced at the hands of others, they in their ignorance did the best they could do, I always say my parents did the best they could with the knowledge they had. You have greater knowledge now and part of self-mastery is letting go of what is not working for you. As you work through the levels you will come to points when you have to let go of self-limiting beliefs and experiences that are holding you back.

Use your mental muscles and the other tools and strategies in this book to help you, if you cannot do it alone find a good life coach who can get you past the mental blocks and take you forward to greater opportunities and achievement.

Chapter Ten

ᘓᕲ

SPIRITUAL OR UNIVERSAL LAWS

You live in a world that is governed by laws, spiritual laws, universal laws, and the laws of the land you live in. The laws of the land can be changed; they are laws that are put there to help you to govern your life, to gain order and discipline so that people may live in relative safety, peace and harmony. You will find that the laws of the land will change according to the beliefs of the people at a given time, if the government decide they want to change a law they can with or without the voice of the people backing them.

Universal laws are different; they are laws that have been in place since the creation of the world, since before man ever existed upon the planet. These laws have always been there and they work the same today as they did when the earth was formed and the laws were put in place. It does not matter how you believe the earth came about, these laws are there and they have always been there, they have never changed and never will change, and no matter how hard you try to change them all you can do is learn to work with them. These laws are no respecter of persons, they treat everyone the same, every time, they are irrevocable, which is to say unchanging.

To examine one of the more obvious of these laws let us look at the law of gravity, it doesn't matter who you are, rich, poor, black, white or brown, slim or fat if you jump off the roof of a building you are going to go downwards towards the ground and you are going to hit the ground the same way as everyone else. It is the law and it doesn't work for some and not for others it works for everyone exactly the same. You can learn to work within this law, which is to respect the law and abseil from the building. The universal law is still working but you are using tools to help you work with the law in being able to jump off the building safely. As a mother you know about this law and that is why you go to great lengths to ensure your children stay within the bounds of this law. You use window locks to stop them jumping or falling out of windows, you use stair gates to stop them falling down stairs. You recognise this law and the importance of living within this law.

The human race has learned to work with these laws and to harness the power of them to help us to live with greater convenience and happiness. These laws are unchanging; if you respect them and work with them they can help you to live a life of joy and harmony.

The laws of time and space are obvious laws that you need to learn to work with. Everyone has 24 hours of time each day, and it is what you do with that time that makes the difference in your life. Each person has various things they need to do each day depending upon their work and their circumstances. You as a mother will have varying circumstances, some of you will be held to a schedule of school times and other class or group times you belong to and you will work your life around these. You will also have an amount of space and again this will be different for everyone. If you learn to use your time and space wisely you can find that they will bring order into your life and in turn this will bring you happiness.

You cannot change the amount of time you have, it is irrevocable, all you can do is to learn to use it better, you cannot change the amount of space you have unless you acquire more space, you can only use the space you have wisely so that you make the most of it. These laws are part of the world you live in and are there to help you to make your life better and happier. When you learn to live within the laws and to use them better you will find that they are good and helpful to you.

Some other universal laws are not so obvious and you may not recognise them as laws and therefore you may not be living your life in harmony with them and that is why you may be finding life is not so happy and is not giving you what you desire. One of these laws is the law of cause and effect, it is a law that affects everyone in the same way, no matter who you are or where you are, this law will affect you the same as everyone else. Imagine putting your hand into a fire, this is a cause, your hand gets burned, this is the effect, and this effect happens to everyone who puts their hand into a fire, they get burned. No amount of money, privilege or anything else you may have to barter with will make any difference, you will get burned if you put your had in a fire.

If in your life you are not getting the results you are seeking then you will not be working in harmony with the law of cause and effect, if you do what you need to do you will get the effect. Some people will say they want to be healthy but they are not willing to live within the health law to bring about this effect. They still want to eat all the rich foods, take no exercise and still be healthy, this will not happen because to have a healthy body it needs to be fed regularly with good wholesome food that will keep the inside of the body working well, as it will keep the outside of the body looking well. The body needs exercise to ensure the organs work as they should and that the sediment from the food is pushed through the system and not allowed to clog up our arteries.

In today's technological world we know that everything vibrates and with this vibrating it moves in waves through the air, like radio waves, microwaves and other forms of vibration that allow radio and television, telephones and internet to work. The ability to be able to talk to someone on the other side of the world and get connected in a few seconds is brought about by harnessing the power of the universal law of vibration.

All of these universal laws work together in harmony, the law of vibration works with the law of cause and effect in perfect harmony. When you make a phone call, (the cause,) you will be connected and speak with the person on the other end no matter where they are, (the effect,) it is the law of vibration that has allowed this to happen.

Another law that can help you in your life is the law of polarity, this law says there is an opposite in everything, if there is an 'in' there must be an 'out' an 'up' and 'down', 'hot' and 'cold', or 'good' and 'bad', everything will have an opposite to it and there will be varying degrees within that opposite. Let us take water as an example; water is made up of two parts hydrogen and one part oxygen and it stays that way no matter what happens to it. So if you make water really cold it will freeze and become solid, it is still water. You have just slowed down the vibration of that water, here the law of vibration is used, now if you take some heat and put it on the ice it will start to vibrate faster and that will cause it to melt and if you keep the heat there it will start to get warmer and vibrate faster until it is boiling water and vibrating at a much higher rate until it turns into steam and then vapour, when this happens it then cools down and becomes water again. So the law of polarity is that you can take the same thing and see how varying degrees of heat or cold or positive or negative can make a difference to it.

It is the same with your thoughts and ideas, they come and go upon the laws of vibration and as you change your thoughts and become more positive and happy you are vibrating at a much higher rate and your energy and enthusiasm levels rise with you. When you start to think negative thoughts you start to cool down and find moving slower and your body will feel heavier, this is how the law of vibration works.

One way you can use this law is within relationships, if you have a relationship with someone that is bad, the law of polarity says that it can be good. You need to draw a line and see where you are on the scale of the relationship.

If your relationship on the scale is over on the bad side you can look at the person and find something good within them and then you can focus your attention on the good thing about the person, this will affect how you feel about the person and help you to build a better relationship with them. The law of polarity says there is good and bad in everyone, this is undisputable, it is a law that is the same for everyone so if you are having trouble with a relationship you can use the law of polarity to help you to build a better relationship.

It may be that one of your children is not as amenable as they use to be, children change especially as they get older and as a mother you have to work within that change and change along with it. As children start to reach teenage years they are thinking and feeling for themselves, they are developing their own values and they may not always be what you value. It is important to continue to see this child as an individual and to accept that they may not always see things the way you do. You must keep your relationship strong by focusing on the good within the child and your relationship with the child.

For you to create the life you desire for yourself and your family you will need to know and understand the universal laws and how they work within your life.

As a person you are a dual entity, meaning there is a physical side to you and a spiritual side, as you learn to work within the laws to create the life you desire you will find that the spiritual side of you is being changed and that is affecting the physical reality of life. It is easy to work with the physical side because you can see it and feel it, you know it is real, but what about the spiritual side, that is something that you can feel within you, it is the part that operates the physical side.

Unfortunately in today's society so much emphasis is put upon the physical body and how it looks and feels that we are not focused on the part of us that can actually change the physical side of us. You see many adverts in the media that focus you on having this perfect body with no wrinkles or blemishes; you are made to feel that if you haven't got the perfect body it is not good.

In actual fact it is what you are on the inside that makes a difference to how you look on the outside. From the outside you probably feel that you should have a perfect 36-24-36 hour glass figure, well, I know for me, that is impossible because I am pear shaped and I cannot change my shape. If on the inside I am thinking I am not good enough because I do not have the perfect figure then the way I am thinking about this will affect my life greatly. If on the other hand I put my focus on the spiritual side of me and decided to change my thinking instead of my body then I would find life so much more rewarding and happier.

How can you make such a change in your life?

Stop and take the time to listen to yourself, to feel your spirit within you and how it feels and what it is saying to you. Everyone has a spirit and everyone's spirit talks to them, when you have this feeling that something is not right or something is missing, when you have the feeling there must be more to life than this, now that is your spirit speaking to you and helping you to look further than the physical. Be prepared to turn off the TV, Radio or other media that is filling your mind everyday with stuff that may not be helping you. Many times you allow your mind to be filled with opinions and information from the media. Then you try to change your life to fit in with the information you are being fed. This is other people trying to tell you how to run your life.

Imagine you have been out of your home and you have come back to find someone has dumped a load of rubbish in your front garden, you question who would do such a thing and you set about cleaning it up. The next day you go out again and when you come home the same thing has happened; you have a load of rubbish on your front garden. This time of course you are really upset and wonder who would do such a thing and you set about cleaning it up again. The next day the very same thing happens but there is more rubbish than before, this time you are really cross and after you clean it up you decide to guard your garden to ensure no one puts rubbish on your garden again.

You could use this as an analogy to what you allow to happen to you everyday that is as you are living your life each day you take in lots of information. A lot of it will be rubbish that is given out by what you watch or listen to via the media. If you take in all the rubbish they give you, as you interact with others and you take in everything that they say to you and you let all this rubbish and other peoples' opinions affect your life and direct your thinking, you find yourself in the circumstances you are in today.

You can cultivate your own mind to think what you want to think and to feel what you want to feel, you decide which values you will have to guide your life, and you decide what you will read and listen to and how it will affect your life. Take control of your mind, remember your body is not the governing part of you and it will be a great benefit to your body when you have cultivated your mind to take over the controls of your life and to create the garden (life) you desire.

Use the spiritual ability you have to walk the path of life you decide, everyone has the right to choose their own way and walk their own path, the other consideration is to walk your path and to allow others the privilege of walking the path of their choice. Do not be swayed by every whim of pleasure or whatever is attractive, sometimes it pays to go without and to take the harder road, be strong and walk your own path to your own tune. Step out of the masses and enjoy your own view and your own bright place in life, and you can take your children with you and build a good foundation for them to build their own life upon.

Remember, what you are thinking all daylong is having a great affect upon your life. You will not be thinking idleness while working industriously to build a nice home for your family. You will not be thinking angry thoughts and smiling sweetly at your child. Remember your children will follow your example so what you want to see in your child needs to be what you are giving out. A child will not grow in confidence if they live with criticism, they need to be nourished and encouraged.

You are a mother and have the greatest opportunity to affect the lives of your children, you can give them every opportunity this life has to offer by giving them an example of living a life that is in harmony with your values and is not affected by outside influences that do not build character.

Part Three

∞

CREATE YOUR FUTURE

I N parts one and two you have learned about who you are and what
you want, you have an understanding of how your mind works to
bring about the life you desire. In this part of the book you are going to
see where you are now in your life and then decide where you want to
be. Then you can make a plan on how you are going to get there.

You have in the previous chapters all the information you need to
change your life and to go in any direction you desire. As a mother I am
sure your direction will include your children.

It is in this section of the book that you will make the greatest progress and therefore be of the greatest benefit to your children. Life is an
opportunity to be the best you can be, to feel the excitement and enthusiasm of life as you change and as you can see your change making
a difference to your children.

Do not give up on this part, you are at the foot of the mountain but
that mountain will shrink in size as you start to make small changes in
your life. Don't get overwhelmed and think you cannot do it, you can,
put your mind to it and take the small steps to change.

Go at your own pace, do not compare yourself to anyone else because you are unique, there is no one else in the world like you, you
have your own values and beliefs that affect your thoughts, feelings and
actions and therefore your results.

Don't get discouraged if something doesn't work the first time, try
again and again until it does work, remember whatever you learn new
needs to be practised and that is what you are doing, practising.

You are special, all mothers are special and you are different, enjoy
that difference, don't try to be the same as others, walk your own road

to the beat of your own drum and have a great time doing it. Your children will love you for it and will respond to your positive changes in life in a positive way.

Chapter Eleven

☙

PRESENT STATE TO DESIRED STATE

LIFE holds three great questions, Who am I? Why am I here? Where am I going? From a spiritual point of view the answers to these questions can be powerful and can give more meaning to a life. I have strong spiritual beliefs that I will set forth in this book to help anyone who is looking for spiritual answers to these questions. It is for you to find your own answers to these questions and how they can affect your life.

Who am I?

I know I am a child of God, the God who created this earth for me to live on, I know I lived with God before I came to this earth and that I had a spiritual existence before this earthly one. I was born into a family where I was taught character building values and given spiritual beliefs that have guided my life. I know that God continues to guide my life as I strive to live in such a way that brings about His purpose for His children to be happy and to grow and learn to develop their spiritual attributes.

Why am I here?

When I lived as a spirit child of God in Heaven I grew and learned new things and I developed a personality that guided my life. I then needed a body to learn even more ways in which I could develop my character and become more like the Father of my spirit. Having a body is helping me to develop a strong character by having to control the physical side of me. My spirit is in control and I can develop patience, tolerance, kindness and other good character traits that help me to become more than I was as a spirit person. As I learn to master my thoughts, words and deeds I am becoming the person my Spiritual

Father in Heaven would have me become and I am succeeding at the purpose for which I have come to this earth.

Where am I going?

My goal is to live this life in accordance with the beliefs and knowledge I have been given and to one day go back and live with my Heavenly Father again. This life is a journey and as I travel this road I can be happy in the knowledge that I know who I am, why I am here, and where I am going. You too can find out the answers to these questions, to do so you will need to ask the questions, you will need to give thought to your own beliefs and also to what you want to know.

These are my beliefs and I have come to the answers after much searching and study because I wanted to know the answers.

Having looked at the spiritual answers to these questions we can now look at the way these questions can give us the guidance and direction we need to get through this earth life.

Who am I?

When you ask this question you may come up with various answers such as: Mother, Daughter, Sister, Wife, Teacher, Housekeeper, and many other roles that you as a woman take on in your life. You are an individual with your own mind and your own feelings and you can use your mind and feeling to direct your life and to have the experiences that will fulfil your needs to learn and progress along this life.

Who am I can also take in the beliefs you have that guide and direct your life along the path it is going? Another question you could ask is Who do I want to be? Take the time to ask these questions often during your day, give life a fair chance by seeking answers to its questions. Asking the question 'who do I want to be?' will open your mind to possibilities, not to sure fired answers but to possibilities. One of the greatest things about life is that it is changeable; you can change something if you need to. You will need to take into account your circumstances and also consequences, if you feel you want to change the circumstance of being married and having children that is something you will need to consider very carefully.

When you get married you make a commitment to someone else and in all your decisions you need to consider that person, when you have a child you again are making a further commitment to another person, to one who will be dependent upon you for a long time. These are the consequences of your decisions and actions and you will need to live with them. A spouse and a child are people with feelings and needs and cannot easily be discarded without great upset and life changing effects.

If you are finding life is not what you would like it to be do not necessarily think that changing the outer circumstances will be the answer because, for many who have tried it have found it did not change the problems they were having because they still did not deal with the inner feelings that were causing them to feel unhappy.

If you are not happy with your life and the way it is, look within you to find the answers before you make decisions that you may live to regret at a later date. Take the time to understand your feelings and why you are feeling this way, know that with a simple change of attitude, this means to view your life from a different perspective you could find your circumstances become much happier and your life is changed without changing the outer circumstances. Work first upon the inner feelings and that will affect how you act on the outside.

Choosing your thoughts carefully can affect the words you speak and the actions you take and you can bring your life into harmony with who you are and help you to find who you want to be.

Why am I here?

Why are you here at this point in your life with the circumstances you have?

From being born you have had experiences in life that have moulded your beliefs and directed your life. Those experiences have brought you to the place you are at in life at this time. When I was young I was brought up to believe as a woman my life would be to get married, have children and to look after those children and also parents, this was the expectation given to me and when I woke up to my life and what was happening to me I found myself married with six children, I was also looking after my mother in law who lived with us because of ill-health.

I lived up to every expectation that was given to me in my experience of life, I was given certain beliefs by my parents and other well meaning adults and I lived up to them. That is how strong your beliefs can be, you will have been given some empowering beliefs and you may also have been given some limiting beliefs. An empowering belief is one that gives you the power to go forward and to fulfil your potential, a self limiting belief is one that stops you from being who you really are because of fear and doubt that you can achieve it.

So why are you here at this point in your life?

The experiences and beliefs you were given as a child have brought you to this point in life, you may also have some beliefs that you have taken on board as an adult and you have been swayed by other peoples' opinions.

An example of this might be my experience at the school gate and hearing other mothers talk about the dreaded school holidays. I would listen to this and take on board their feelings and make them mine, I would dread the school holidays because the children would be home under my feet all day. Now how did that make me feel? It made me feel negative towards my children, I saw them has a hindrance and a chore, I didn't really feel that way about my children but taking on someone else's opinion gave me those thoughts and feelings.

Then one day I said something to someone else about the dreaded school holidays and they said they looked forward to them because it gave them the freedom from a schedule, it gave them the freedom to go out and not be tied to a time of returning. Now I have a different opinion, a much more positive one that enables me to see my children not as a hindrance but as an opportunity to learn and to grow and to develop circumstances that would bring happiness to all of us. So I develop my own opinion based on my feelings and my desires, I do not have to listen and go with anyone else's thoughts about life and how it should be, I am an independent person walking my own path and therefore it is my opinions that count and no one else's.

So why am I here, because this is where my thoughts, my words and my actions have brought me and they will take me along the path of life to where I am going.

Where am I going?

I am going exactly where my thoughts, words and action are taking me. How careful you should be to choose your thoughts, they will affect your emotions/feelings and they will also affect the way your body reacts to your thought stimulation.

Some questions you could ask here are: Where do I want to go? What do I want?

Asking questions will help your mind to think and to help you to create positive change in your life. Asking the right questions can bring you amazing breakthroughs that will help you to develop circumstances that will make a positive difference in your life.

When you ask the right questions you will steer clear of the Why me? Why does nothing ever go right for me?

Some better questions you could ask would be:

What do I want?

What needs to happen now?

What is my aim in life?

How can I make a difference?

These questions will guide you through to find answers that will help you to create the life you want. When you ask questions you are inviting answers and the answers to positive questions will give you the needed guidance and direction you are looking for.

What do I want?

This is a basic question that many people just do not know the answer to. As you ask this question, not just once but giving it time and opportunity, ask it many times and you will find the answer. So ask yourself the question now and see what your mind is drawn to. You may say I want to be happy, that's good as that is what most of us want, now you can ask the next question, what will make me happy? This is a question that needs great thought, to say more money or better health will then bring other questions that will create more questions and also eventually require some commitment from you.

You can see that asking one question will lead you along a path that as you travel it you will find more questions and more answers and as you find the answers and take the necessary actions you will be creating a life that you desire to live. It is important that you check to make sure the path you are treading is leading to where you want to go.

Now we have answered the three greatest questions from a physical sense you need a plan, a system you can work with to ensure you travel your own road and not someone else's. You need a plan to ensure you make progress and do not get back onto that road that is travelled by the masses. Always beware of falling back on to this road, remember how hard it was to push your way off it and you do not want to get sucked back on to it again.

What needs to happen now?

There can come a time in your life when you are so busy that important things that you want or need to do don't get done and you can feel swamped or overwhelmed. Sometimes in life you can be going along and everything seems to be going okay until you realise that there are certain things that are not getting done. It may be a project that you have started and then you were distracted and now you are running behind time with the project.

This can start to affect your life, it maybe affecting your sleep and other parts of your life until you feel you are living with a lead weight around your neck and you are held bound by it.

At a time like this you can develop a plan to get your project under way again and working toward a conclusion. There is a simple four-step plan that will help you.

1. Write down what outcome you desire.
2. Write down where you are at present.
3. Draw a path between the two.
4. Mark the steps you need to take on the path.

You can then follow the path you have drawn fulfilling each step along the way, the size of the project will determine how long and how many steps there are in the pathway you are following.

It does not matter what it is from carrying out a domestic chore to fulfilling a project at work, this simple formula will help you to know what needs to happen next.

What is my aim in life?

Your aim in life can be answered by what you want to do in your life, but will more likely be what you see as your purpose in life. To know your purpose and then to follow it through to fulfilment you will need to take quiet time to think about what you want and then what you intend to do. These can be different things because we can very often want something but have no intention of doing what it takes to get it.

Your aim or purpose will be important to you and you will have the intention of following it. Take time each day to be quiet and to notice what is happening around you, give 100% of your attention to what is going on around you and start to become more aware of what is in your life. Many people do not give this attention and go through life each day missing important information and opportunity.

Now you are beginning to know what is already in your life and what you are feeling you will be in a better position to decide what your purpose or aim is in life. Becoming aware of you and your surrounding life may take sometime, the more you can give to this the more you will become aware of what is happening and what you want to happen. Don't try to rush this, you have the rest of your life to achieve it and it will be much easier if you choose the right pathway first, so become much more aware of you and your life. When you feel you are reaching some conclusions in your awareness, you can then use the simple plan laid out in the last question to design a pathway to achieving your aim in life.

How can I make a difference?

The world we live in is a changing world, almost with each year that comes things change and life becomes more and more complex, this can very often give the feeling of being swallowed up in the process of what is happening in the world around you.

Asking yourself how I can make a difference will open your mind up to possibilities; it will bring opportunity to your door as you become more aware of what is happening around you. Keep asking yourself this question until one day you will find that small step by small step you have made a difference somewhere in life.

When you ask questions such as these you will come up with answers, your sub conscious will furnish the answers for you and it will be a matter of you following through on the promptings you receive.

You may have a talent of some kind and as you ask the question on how you can make a difference you could be prompted to use your talent in a way that will make a difference, not only to yourself but to the people around you, in the community, running a group teaching them what you know or just working one on one with other people to lift and inspire them in their lives.

Ask the question several times each day and then go forward and do what you feel is going to make a difference to you and to others around you.

Having these questions and seeking answers to them will help you to know who you are now and where you want to go, what future you want to create for yourself and those around you. It does not matter who you are now or who you think you are it is what you desire and where you desire to be that are important. As you work upon this you can change and develop until you feel you have moved toward the desired state you had in your plans for your life.

As a mother you will set a great example to your children as you create the life you want. You will bring harmony into your life as you start to live the values you have in your life. Your children will see purpose and direction in your life that will help them to feel stability and have a greater understanding of what they can achieve in their life.

Do not under estimate the affect your involvement with life can have on your children, when I was a young child my mother was ill and could not contribute very much to the community I was part of. I had friends in that community whose mothers were very much a part of what was going on, they organised and participated in all the activities and this also involved my friends. I on the other hand was always on the outside watching from a distance and wanting to be part of it but not being a part of it.

This served to diminish my confidence and my ability to perform within my community. Had my parents been there and involved, I might have had the confidence to be there too. A parent can make a difference in their child's life by being part of the community the child is part of, whether that is at school or any other community project it will greatly help your child's confidence to know you are interested and want to be part of what they are.

You will greatly benefit from getting involved in anything you are interested in; it will build your confidence and give you new insights into yourself and what you want out of life. Keep asking yourself questions and seeking answers, this will open up your mind to greater possibilities than you have at present. The greater the questions the greater the possibility and the greater the plan you will need to carry forward some of these possibilities.

You are the most important person in the world, in your world and in your child's world; you are the heart of your family and as such need to be beating to your own rhythm. As you do you will start to feel the difference that knowing who you are and what your purpose is can make in your life. You will start to feel more involved in life, develop more confidence and the ability to know and understand yourself and how you can achieve your ambitions. Be your own best friend and talk to yourself in a way that lifts and inspires you to take the next small step upon the path of happiness. It is your right to be happy, as it is your child's right to be happy, feel this happiness grow and spread as you start to realise your potential as a mother and an individual who can make a difference to the world around them.

As you take upon yourself the responsibility to be happy and to provide a place of peace and understanding for your child to be happy in, you will grow and develop in a way that you never thought possible, you will start to realise your potential and become the person you always were but had been locked away behind self-imposed prison bars of self-limiting belief.

See where you are on the road to happiness and use this knowledge to develop your plan, look at your child and ask yourself, does this child deserve to be happy? Everyone deserves to be happy, no matter what he or she does, how he or she feels and how you feel about him or her. It matters not their age, all desire happiness as much as you do, they will need your help to find it and develop it in their lives.

If you are feeling a little overwhelmed by this, I know that if you have been living with the masses, on the level of thought and emotion of the masses it can be quite a daunting thought to think and feel on an individual basis, do not let this stop you, go at your own pace and make small changes, even infinitely small changes. An example of this could be that you have a relationship with one of your children that is not as good as it could be, maybe you are angry with each other and it could be that you do not know how to break that cycle you have in your relationship. Start small with a smile every so often or biting your tongue and not retorting with an angry comment.

Do not think you have to change your world overnight, be patient with yourself and the people around you, and remember that they will need time to respond to you and your efforts to bring light and happiness into the lives of all.

Chapter Twelve

☙

PLAN OF HAPPINESS

ANY happiness you have in this world will come because your attitude is attuned to it. With the right attitude you can achieve all you desire.

If you ask any people what they want out of life their reply will usually fall into one of three categories, health, wealth and happiness. If you want to live a life that is fulfilled and where you feel you have made a difference then you will need to feel that you have or are achieving a level of happiness that is giving you satisfaction and is rewarding.

First of all let us define what happiness is; it is this deep sense of well being, good spirits and cheerfulness, where you can feel at peace with yourself, you know you are doing your best, you know what is happening around you because you know who you are and what your purpose is. To be happy is more than being able to laugh and have great joy all the time, it is more than heady excitement and doing things all the time that are making you smile and laugh. To be happy is about your life being a great adventure, it is a way of living that will give you cause to say 'I have lived a good life.'

Being happy is still having that deep sense of well being even when hard times come, when things are not going so well or you are under some pressure. When this happens to a happy person they do not immediately lose their happiness and become depressed, they will know that this is transitory and it will come to pass and their happiness will not be changed because of it.

Happiness is a habit that you will need to develop in your life as with any habit it will take time and practise to get it to a point where it becomes automatic and you are naturally happy everyday. When you choose the happiness habit you are choosing to think and act in a happy way.

Many people chase happiness in the form of money and power only to find that when they have them they are not any happier than they were before. Happiness is a state of mind and everyone can have it, whether rich or poor, black or white, as a person you are entitled to be happy, you are born with equal rights and there is no embargo on happiness, it is yours for the choosing.

Living in the western world with all the conveniences of the world you would think people would be the happiest on earth but sadly that is not true, it seems people are chasing happiness everywhere, spending vast amounts of money to find it and still missing it somehow. There is more depression than happiness, there are more people taking drugs to make them happy, people can't even find happiness in marriage, more than half of them end in divorce. Why?

Happiness is something that has to be nurtured and developed, it does not come immediately with a smile, it comes when you have decided you are going to be happy and you are going to see the happy side of your life everyday. An attitude of 'eat, drink and be merry for tomorrow we die' will not help you to find happiness. That will only increase your unhappiness because of the instability of what tomorrow may bring and whether you will be able to cope with it. You can plan your happiness just as you can plan your meals; it is planning for the future, for your future happiness. Make sure happiness is part of your daily planned activity, you can be happy by seeing happiness all around you and in every situation.

People are not finding happiness because they are chasing the wrong thing; they are looking to the outside world for happiness, collecting more 'toys', trying to be more popular, to be rich, to be thin, to have the right job, to be good looking enough and finally when they have all these things they will live happily ever after.

Lives are filled everyday with activities, and when you rush from one to another, on an adrenaline rush you can mistake the high you receive as happiness, only to find you have to keep doing more and more to give that feeling, that high you think is happiness.

One of the most important things you will learn about happiness is that it has nothing to do with anything on the outside of you, nothing, not winning the lottery or having everything you could wish for will bring you happiness.

Happiness is a choice; and your genes or your environment or up-bringing does not determine it. These things can have a strong influence on you but will not determine whether you are happy or not, you will still have the choice to be happy.

The story is told of twin brothers, one of them grew up to be an alcoholic and the other to be a successful businessman. When the alcoholic was asked why he became a drunk, he replies, "My father was a drunk." When the successful businessman was asked why he became successful, he says, "My father was a drunk." Same background. Same upbringing. Different choices.

Each day we live, events are happening to us and we are responding to them, our response to these events is critical, think of the twins one responded to the events in his life by feeling hopeless and giving up. The other responded by saying, "I am not going to let that happen to me." He worked and became successful. You have the choice on how you respond to everyday events in your life, you may not always have control of the events but you do have control over how you will respond to those events. There are many times when you do not realise you are making a choice because the speed of your reaction to the event.

The first step in achieving happiness is to realise that you are making choices, everyday; all day you are making choices that are affecting your life. You are making choices as to how you will respond to any given situation even if you are not aware of these choices you are still making them, and the choice you make will decide whether your happiness is increased or decreased. Once you start to recognise that you are making choices you will then start to gain power over some of your responses.

Imagine your child is acting up and this is having the affect of making you feel irritable, your child continues with this behaviour until you lose your temper with them and shout and rant at them, then you say to them 'now see what you made me do.' The child did not make you lose your temper, you chose to do that, you could also have chosen to walk out of the room until you could control how you were feeling.

This is where you get to choose your responses, you get to decide what will happen and your response will decide if you are happier or unhappier because of the situation. Awareness of what is happening around you will play a big part in creating a happy life, you will be aware of situations that need a response and if you have developed habits that will bring you happiness you will not have to stop and think at every situation but you will be in the habit of making choices that will bring happiness.

So choosing to be happy and to make a habit of it means choosing to respond to everyday situations in ways that will bring long-term happiness rather than letting your automatic, unthinking responses take over and destroy any chance you have of being happy. To become a happy person you can learn characteristics and traits that will consistently bring you happiness and if you are happy you will find that you have a sense of control over your life, you are optimistic, you will like yourself as a person, and you will be confident and outgoing. Another thing you will have is a purpose, happy people will have a purpose that is higher than them and you will strive to do things that make a positive difference to your world.

As part of your plan of happiness you can use your own mind to develop your happiness, remember the six mental muscles you have to help you to control your mind and how you respond to life. You have:

1. Perception, this will help you to view your life from the viewpoint of happiness.

2. Imagination, this will help you to visualise what can be and create it.

3. Willpower, to help you to focus and concentrate to bring about the life you desire.

4. Intuition, this feeling will be your guide and help you know which direction to take.

5. Memory will be there to assist you to learn and grow from your experiences.

6. Reasoning, to know you have a choice and that you can reason as to which choice you want.

The purpose of your life is not to endure it in misery or pain, the purpose of life is joy and happiness, it is to learn to use the abilities you have been given and to make wise choices that will give you everything you desire, you can be, do or have whatever you are willing to create in your life.

Everyone has the same tools given to them to help them create a life of happiness, it is just that some people have used and developed these tools more than others so you get people on varying levels of happiness and success.

Choose to be happy and make a habit of it, you have a divine right to be happy and no one can take that right from you. Right thinking and acting is where you will start to develop your happiness, let us look at right thinking.

Examine your own thinking, at this moment now, are you thinking or is your mind just busy? There is a difference, your mind can be very busy with all sorts of thoughts flitting in and out at lightening speed, and do any of them stay long enough for you to really think about them. Try this experiment; focus your mind on the door handle of the room you are in right now, think about this door handle and time yourself doing it. How long did you focus your thoughts on it before another thought came in? Probably a few seconds, if you are not used to focused concentration of thought it is something you can develop so you can have the choice of thinking right thoughts.

Thousands of thoughts pass through your mind everyday and although most of these thoughts are unconscious they do have an effect on you because of the action you took based on them. Your thoughts and reactions come so fast that it seems that this is what life is and you don't actually experience actively choosing anything. If you want to be happy you need an awareness of the choices you are making, in that way you will gain control over how you respond to those thoughts instead of an automatic response.

In today's world you can fall into the trap of responding negatively to what is happening around you, seeing other people's behaviour as a negative intent and also worrying about things that may or may not happen, this kind of thinking can have a way of consuming you and making you think you have no control. This is where depression and other conditions can creep in and take over your life, this is not right thinking and you can change that, you have the choice to think in a different way and to get past this negative thinking that does not serve you.

Let me tell you about a situation that arose between two of my children. My daughter was in her middle teens and was developing her own outlooks on life; she also had a younger brother who was almost 7 years her junior. As you can imagine there were times when this younger brother would do things that would irritate her and wind her up, this may have happened more than a little as he would have enjoyed the response he got from it. One day when my daughter was about 17 she came to me with a concern that every time she saw her young brother she felt this great irritation rise up inside of her, he didn't have to do anything, just walk into the same room. This irritation would rise in her and it started to bother her. She loved her brother even if he did wind her up and it concerned her that she should feel this way. After some effort she learned to control her own thinking and to look past his childlike behaviour and to see his good points, this helped her to have a different relationship with him that was able to grow and mature and she was much happier with it.

It takes effort to focus your mind on what you want but if you keep doing it you will develop the habit and it will become automatic to be happy and to make happy choices. Think about situations in your own life where if you chose to think differently about it you could bring happiness into your life, think about your children and how you respond to them, sometimes you may expect certain behaviour and then get it whereas if you had expected something different you may have got that too. Your children will give you what you want if they know what you want and you let them know you expect it from them.

Following closely behind right thinking is right acting, to act in a way that will lift and inspire you and others around you, to act in a way that you have peace of mind and to be able to hold your head up and know you did your best. Doing the right thing will be doing that which will bring you happiness and peace of mind. Not guilt and sorrow for actions taken that you wish you could take back.

As a mother your greatest work will be with your children and I don't know any mother who doesn't want her child to be happy, confident and to have joy. This will not come to your child if you do not have it, you are their example, and they will follow you and what you do. You have the greatest and happiest work on the planet, you have the opportunity to make a difference to your child, you can learn and develop your own happiness and naturally pass this on to the child or you can sit back and let nature take its course and run the risk of your child finding its own happiness. The problem with the latter choice is that the child may have to learn some very hard lessons that will cause much heartache for you and them whilst they are learning, and even then they may never find happiness.

Make being happy your number one priority, when you are happy the people around you will be happy, you have that privilege of affecting the lives of others. I grew up being taught that the mother of the home was the heart of the home and if you were asked where is happiness you would probably touch your heart and say this is where happiness is. I know it is not always easy to be the happy one but when you make it a habit you will automatically display happiness, it is just sticking with the effort of changing your thinking to happy thinking and your acting to happy acting. It will be so worth it and you do not have to wait long to see the results, from the minute you start to make changes to your thinking and acting you will see results happening.

I will always remember my daughter saying to me when she was about 10 years old, 'you don't smack us anymore do you mummy?' I had learned a different way, I had learned to control my thinking and acting and the way I viewed their behaviour to be able to respond in a different way. This had the effect of my children responding in a different way and their behaviour changing too. When one-thing changes it will have a ripple effect and change many things, see the stone being dropped into the water and causing ripples, as each ripple goes out it touches other things and has an affect on them. It is the same with you and your child or children, when you change one small thing it will have a ripple affect and change other things.

You can build happiness into your life everyday by building habits of happiness, to do this you will need to understand three things that will help you to build the happiness habit, they are:

1. To appreciate what you already have

2. To continue to learn and to grow personally

3. The ability to respond effectively to situations.

Your ability to do the three things above will affect the level of happiness you can achieve. To appreciate what you already have is to be grateful for it and to acknowledge that gratitude by being happy with what you already have, you could write down all the things you are grateful for and also everyday make a habit at the end of each day writing down the things that have happened during the day that you were grateful for. This will have the effect of helping you to realise that you do already have a certain amount of happiness in your life and when you write down other things that are happening daily you will realise how much your happiness is growing. An example of what you may write might be how grateful you are for the beautiful smile one of your children gave you when you helped them. Some of the things that make us happy are not physical but they are emotional and spiritual.

YOUR DAILY PLAN OF HAPPINESS
Upon Awakening:

Spend one minute before you get out of bed being grateful for being alive and having another day to choose to be happy.

During this time visualise yourself being happy as you go about doing your normal everyday activities. Affirm to yourself 'I am happy and I choose to be happy in my work and play.'

Next read something inspiring for ten minutes, something that will motivate you and help you to choose happiness as a habit.

Having previously decided which level of self-mastery you are at, choose something you can do during the day that will help you to attain the next level of self-mastery.

If you are at the level of the masses and you want to move to the level of aspiration then you can choose to do this, as you take the time each morning be grateful and visualise yourself doing your everyday activities, visualise yourself aspiring to a higher level of living. If you aspire to be more in control of your actions then visualise a situation where you choose to act in a way different to your normal reaction.

To make any change in your life is not hard; it is a matter of doing it until it becomes habit. It can be something small that will make a big difference. Like being a little more organised, putting the hairbrush in a certain place so you will know where it is in the morning when you are late for school and your child's hair needs brushing. This may seem like a small thing but the chaos it can cause can be large, I remember this from when my children were young and I had two daughters with long hair and if I couldn't find the hairbrush it caused friction and panic. This in turn caused thoughts and feelings that left you wondering if it was all worth it.

Ask yourself is my happiness worth the effort it will take to have it in my life?

When you look around you at the world and what is happening in it, are you moved and inspired to want to bring a little happiness in to the lives of others. Sometimes you can think that it is not worth it, you cannot make any difference to things that are happening in the world. Think on a much smaller scale, see your little part of the world and determine to bring happiness to that, if everyone decided to make their own little part of the world happy the world would change and there would be happiness everywhere, people would love and be kind to one another and it would make the world a better place to live, especially for your child.

In the evening you can take the time to mentally go through your day and see how you did, congratulate yourself on the times when you did well and controlled your thoughts. If you did slip accept that when you are learning something new you make mistakes and it is okay to make mistakes. Analyse the situation and look at where you could have done something different and then resolve to do it the right way next time. Do not beat yourself up and make yourself feel bad, that will not help you, it will only serve to keep you bound at the level you are now.

Before you go to sleep affirm your success and your confidence to be more than you are now.

Chapter Thirteen

∽

APPRECIATE 'YOU'

Y OU have a choice about everything in life, you can choose to be courageous and to appreciate the great person you are. It takes courage to go forward and to live the life you desire, it takes courage to create your own life, to lift everything about your life, make it lighter and more enjoyable by being optimistic and know that whatever you are doing whatever you are experiencing can be for your benefit. It can help you to grow in every way and give you a feeling of enthusiasm and energy that can only come when there's a smile on your face and a spring in your step.

The last chapter of this book is about you and how you can appreciate yourself and all the skills and ability you have developed whilst carrying out your everyday life as a mother.

What does it mean to appreciate you?

To show gratitude; thankful recognition to yourself for all the hard work and effort you put into living every day. One way you can do this is through your 'self talk,' through letting that small voice, sometimes known as the inner critic; say words of appreciation and recognition for your efforts.

Many times, especially as mothers you are too hard on yourselves, because there is no 'how to' manual with your child. A lot of your work comes from your intuition and your ability to feel for that child. This is quite amazing and each mother can show great appreciation to herself for doing what is arguably the hardest job in the world with no formal training and manual.

Appreciate yourself and be kind to yourself, even if you feel you are just managing to keep your head above water, pat yourself on the back and acknowledge your endeavours to be the best mother you can be in your present state of knowledge and awareness.

As a mother you are the most important person in your child's life and they will look to you for everything they need, as you appreciate yourself you will also feel an appreciation for your child, and they in turn will feel this appreciation and respond to it with behavior that allows you to appreciate yourself and them, more. So the cycle goes and relationships change and grow and happiness and appreciation become a normal part of everyday life.

How does appreciation work?

When you appreciate something, that is, being grateful for something, you are focusing on what you do, or have, in your life instead of complaining about what you do not have. Your focus is on what you are receiving in your life and the universal laws always work in giving you more of what you focus on. If you are focused on anger that is what you will get and you will keep getting more anger in your life until you start to put your focus upon something else. If you are focused upon being happy in life then you will keep getting more and more happiness that is how life works, it is how it is supposed to work.

There is a saying about appreciation that shows how this works. It is 'Where focus goes energy flows.' This means that where you are putting your focus, the things you are thinking about are the things you will attract into your life. So if you are focused on being happy you will attract more happiness into your life. It works because that is what you are giving out and people naturally respond in a like manner.

This is especially powerful in families; because you are living in close proximity to each other you affect each other greatly. I well remember the mornings when I would lie in bed and say to myself today is going to be a good day, I am not going to get impatient with anyone and I am going to be loving and see each person out of the house in a loving manner. On the whole this worked for me, I am not saying it was not difficult, I had a daughter who did not like anyone to talk to her or bother her too much in the mornings, she was happy to get up and do what she had to do without any interaction from others. Unfortunately she had a brother who knew this and who took every opportunity to irritate her and to make her shout or get upset.

This in turn called for me to step in and to help my son to under-stand that his comments were not necessary. To advise my daughter to let his comments go over the top of her head and not to take them seriously. I would end up being the referee practising and strengthen-ing my powers of patience. This sometimes worked and other times it did not, and I would lose my patience and end up yelling at them. This then would make me ask myself 'is it all worth it?'

So many times when you decide to do or be something that you want to do or be when the challenges come it can be hard to stay fo-cused on what you are trying to accomplish. When you do lose your focus and you revert back to behaviour that you are trying to overcome, you can feel like you have failed, this can have the effect of draining you of your energy and resolve to be better. It is at these times that you need to show some appreciation for yourself and the effort you are making to improve and to become who you really want to be or to do the things you really want to do.

If your challenge and focus is to be kind and patient in the morning and you lose it somewhere along the way, appreciate yourself for even wanting such a high level of endeavour in your life and then appreciate the amount of time you managed to stay kind and patient. Some days you will find that you managed all day to be the person you desired to be and other days you will find that something got too much and you weakened at some point.

Remember life is a journey and as part of that journey there are go-ing to be some miles that are uphill and hard going, these are the parts of the journey that strengthen you, that help to strengthen your heart and your mind to stay focused on the path you are walking.

Being a mother is a big part of your journey and it is the part where you will learn many new talents, skills and abilities that will help you for the rest of your life. One day when your children are older and do not need you as much, you may decide to get a job in the employment market place. The skills and abilities you have learned and developed as a mother will be really useful in your work; you will be able to transfer them from the home to your work place. Such things as organizational skills, budgeting, estimating, design, management and many other things you have been doing in your home whilst raising your children you can now use in the work place to do your job.

If you think of the amount of organisation it takes to run a home, especially if you have more than one child and you have to organise space not only for the children but for their clothes, their toys and books, completing their school work. You also have to organise your time and schedules to ensure you and your children get to school and appointments on time. Without any formal training you have developed organizational skills that you can use anywhere, remember being a mother is more than looking after children.

How many books or magazines have you read about designing your home, or if you did not read any you may have put a lot of effort into the design of your home, from the decorating to where you decided to put your furniture to most effectively serve you and your family. You have more talents and ability now than you did before you decided to become a mother, there will be many ways in which you have grown and developed that will help you in other areas of your life.

Appreciate this, appreciate that every day when you perhaps feel life is a little hard and maybe sometimes boring you have been developing yourself for the next stage of your life, when your children become more independent and don't need you as much. This is what life is all about, I am a great believer in the cycle of life, that you are always moving forward toward another cycle and that when you are ready the time will come for you to move onwards and upwards toward greater joy, happiness and appreciation of who you are, why you are here and where you are going. The three questions with which we started part three of the book and never answered completely because life is an ongoing experience that we can appreciate and enjoy.

Have the greatest life appreciating yourself, your children and your world around you.

ISBN 1425180005-1

9 781425 180058